ASTER OF CEREMONIES

ALSO BY JJJJJEROME ELLIS

The Clearing

multiverse

Series Editor
Chris Martin

Cover Description

The cover of this book shows a hand-drawn illustration of a Plant with pale purple-blue flowers (the word "Plant" is capitalized in this book as a way of showing respect to botanical life). This Plant is known by several names, including Glaucous Aster and *Symphyotrichum laeve*. The drawing was made by the British illustrator Sydenham Edwards (1768–1819). The silhouetted illustration appears over a lavender background with rows of white asterisks that evoke lines of text. Six white rectangles are scattered on the lavender background as well. They bear black text that reads (one word per rectangle): "Aster of Ceremonies Poems JJJJJEROME ELLIS." The cover was designed by Mary Austin Speaker.

ASTER[1] OF CEREMONIES

Some Notes Performed[2] toward a Ceremony[3], containing several Movements of a Hymn—or a Black, Dysfluent[4] Chant—and an Essay for a Liturgy of the Name, Offered in Devotion to Our Kin[5]; in other words, Some Pages of a Reverence[6] Book Awaiting to be Gathered[7] and Sung with other Quires[8]

JJJJJEROME ELLIS

MILKWEED EDITIONS

---

[1] Asters are a group of flowering Plants.

[2] "I've been concerned for a long time with Black performances as the resistance events of persons denied the capacity to claim normative personhood."—Fred Moten

[3] "That which we have made we can unmake and consciously now remake."—Sylvia Wynter, "Ceremony Found"

[4] "Dysfluent" here refers to forms of disabled or non-normative speech, including stuttering/stammering (the two terms are synonomous), aphasia, Tourette's, and others.

[5] ". . . our nonhuman kin are sometimes the family members with the greatest fugitive stance for resistance" —Jennell Navarro and Kimberly Robertson, "The Countdown Remix: Why Two Native Feminists Ride with Queen Bey" in *Otherwise Worlds: Against Settler Colonialism and Anti-Blackness*

[6] Thank you, Luísa Black, for showing me the closeness of *reference* and *reverence*.

[7] "if you don't gather them all you will never be free."—Alexis Pauline Gumbs, *Dub: Finding Ceremony*

[8] Quires are groups of pages gathered to form a bound book.

Published 2023 by Milkweed Editions
Printed in the United States of America
Cover design by Mary Austin Speaker
Cover illustration by Sydenham Edwards
Author photo by Annie Forrest
23 24 25 26 27   5 4 3 2 1
First Edition

Library of Congress Cataloging-in-Publication Data

Names: Ellis, JJJJJerome, author.
Title: Aster of ceremonies : poems / JJJJJerome Ellis.
Description: First edition. | Minneapolis : Milkweed Editions, 2023. | Series: Multiverse |
    Summary: "Aster of Ceremonies asks what rites we need now and how poetry, astir in the
    asters, can help them along"-- Provided by publisher.
Identifiers: LCCN 2023001095 (print) | LCCN 2023001096 (ebook) | ISBN 9781639550128 (trade
    paperback) | ISBN 9781639550135 (ebook)
Subjects: LCGFT: Poetry.
Classification: LCC PS3605.L4665 A88 2023 (print) | LCC PS3605.L4665 (ebook) | DDC
    813/.6--dc23/eng/20230313
LC record available at https://lccn.loc.gov/2023001095
LC ebook record available at https://lccn.loc.gov/2023001096

Milkweed Editions is committed to ecological stewardship. We strive to align our book production practices with this principle, and to reduce the impact of our operations in the environment. We are a member of the Green Press Initiative, a nonprofit coalition of publishers, manufacturers, and authors working to protect the world's endangered forests and conserve natural resources. *Aster of Ceremonies* was printed on acid-free 100% postconsumer-waste paper by Sheridan Saline.

FOR SWAMP HONEYSUCKLE

CONTENTS

give me a speech impediment
that I may live

give me a speech impediment
that I may give
notice

give me a speech impediment
that I may notice
Asters

Aster of Ceremonies

INTRODUCTION

To any readers of this work who stutter, stammer, or otherwise speak dysfluently:

I celebrate and honor your speech.

Seedtime and harvest. Sowing and reaping. My mother Pauline taught my brother Kelvin and I how to think in these terms. Sow kindness, reap kindness. Both my grandmothers, Joan and Etta, love to garden. Etta, who went home in 2012, lined her Brooklyn apartment with Houseplants. In 2022 Joan requested two Thyme Plants in pots, and I had the great privilege of bringing them to her. Her son, my father John, sends me a video of the Chrysanthemums he just planted in his garden. My maternal grandfather Charles was a farmer and minister in Jamaica. I called my mother and asked her what he grew: Yam, Coco, Pear (also known as Avocado), Sweet Potato, Banana, Sugarcane, Squash, Pumpkin, and Cabbage. His father was also a farmer and minister, and his father was a farmer and minister. My dear homie Adjua Gargi Nzinga Greaves writes about Plants with such fierce care and precision. Stutterer Jordan Scott's book *I Talk Like a River* teaches me so much about what the Earth can teach us about stuttering. Ditto for Conor Foran, Patrick Campbell, Kristel Kubart, Ramdeep Roman, Laura Lascău, and Paul Aston—the team behind Making Waves: a Stuttering Pride Flag (thank you for inviting me to dream up this flag with yall!). Ecologist, landscape designer, poet, educator Luísa Black Ellis labors and plays every day in the service of Plants. The African and North American Indigenous ancestors who practiced marronage in the Great Dismal Swamp (where I've learned about some of the Plants found in this book) continue to teach me.

❦

I'll briefly introduce myself. I'm an artist and proud stutterer. I was raised by Jamaican and Grenadian immigrants in Tidewater, Virginia, where I live with my wife, Luísa Black Ellis. Luísa and I got married while this book was being written. In some sections of the book, I refer to her as my best friend, because we weren't married at the time I wrote those sections. She's still my best friend. :)

This book is a series of offerings, traces of practices I've been engaged in for years.

In Part I you'll find six poems. "Octagon of Water, Movement 2," "Movement 3," and "Movement 4" continue a poem that began in my previous book *The Clearing*. "Prayer to My Stutter #2," "#4," and "#6" similarly continue a poem that began as two publications in the online magazine *The Offing*.

In Part II you'll find an essay, "Liturgy of the Name."

In Part III you'll find the beginnings of a hymn called "Benediction."

In Part IV you'll find another essay, "Astering the Stutter."

In Part V you'll find one more movement from "Benediction," as well as "Octagon of Water, Movement 5."

❀

In May 2020, a sentence from sound artist Christof Migone's book *Sonic Somatic* stopped me: "Some statistics indicate a high incidence of stuttering amongst slaves." In a footnote Migone cites historian Michael P. Johnson's article "Runaway Slaves and the Slave Communities in South Carolina, 1799 to 1830." I quickly found the article and encountered there, for the first time, so-called "runaway slave" advertisements.

Throughout the eighteenth and nineteenth centuries, enslavers in the Caribbean, Latin America, Great Britain, and the United States of America placed advertisements in newspapers when the people they were enslaving "ran away." I use scare quotes here to trouble the apparent simplicity of the language used to describe what these enslaved folks were doing, what kinds of movement they were practicing. And as a student of historian Saidiya Hartman, I take seriously her attention to the extremely fraught nature of this archive, and other archives of slavery. Her reflections in her book *Scenes of Subjection* speak to what's happening in *Aster of Ceremonies*: "[T]he documents, fragments, and accounts considered here, although claimed for purposes contrary to those for which they were gathered, nonetheless remain entangled within the politics of domination."

I've wrestled with how to refer to the enslaved in this book. I don't want to erase the reality of their enslavement. At the same time, I seek a word that carries respect and honor, and which encompasses more than the fact of their enslavement. I've chosen to refer to them as enslaved Ancestors, or just Ancestors. Yet these terms feel complicated to me too.

When I came across these advertisements, I was reading the book *Zong!* by poet m. nourbeSe philip, "as told to the author by Setaey Adamu Boateng," the ancestral voice "revealing the submerged stories of all who were on board the [slave ship] *Zong.*" I'm still reading that book, will always be reading it. philip created the text by restricting herself to the words (and anagrams of those words) of an eighteenth century legal decision concerning the massacre of Africans aboard the slave ship *Zong.* Apprenticing myself to this method, I started copying down "runaway slave" advertisements onto a blank sheet of paper every morning. I began to isolate words from the ads to form phrases and sentences. Eventually I found myself focusing on ads that named enslaved Ancestors who stuttered, stammered, or spoke with speech impediments (sometimes referred to as "stoppages" in speech). Lines about stuttering started arising:

Stutters are vessels.

A stutter is a well.

The stutters will be harbours / for years.

I found pleasure writing these lines. Why?

A few years ago I encountered the Greek term *antonomasia*, which refers to ritual or devotional practices of naming and renaming, like listing the names of god or divinities. I find a lot of resonance between those practices and the process of writing these lines. For most of my life I named my stutter Burden, Curse, Disorder, Issue, Problem. But when I write "stutters are vessels," the name Vessel becomes a door that invites me into a new relationship with my stutter. If x is this, what is y? If stutters are vessels, what is my mouth? Is my mouth like one of those glass cases in a museum that holds ancient vessels? If stutters are vessels, what are they carrying? And thus, what am I carrying? I've found a lot of healing in this renaming.

3

As I spent more time with these advertisements, I came across another archive: *The Flora of North America*, an encyclopedic guide to the native and naturalized plants of North America north of Mexico. Flipping through the dozen or so volumes of the *Flora* at Old Dominion University's Perry Library in Norfolk, Virginia, I grow intoxicated reading the names of different Plants: *Ranunculus*, Daisy-leaf Moonwort, *Symphyotrichum*, *Matelea*.

I became curious about bringing these two archives into contact: "runaway slave" advertisements concerning dysfluent Ancestors and *The Flora of North America*. The ads are typically brief (two hundred words or less) and brutally to-the-point: name of the enslaved, name of the enslaver, physical description of the enslaved (including the clothes they were wearing when last seen), a reward amount, and a warning against harboring the "fugitive". The *Flora* is projected to run to thirty volumes (it's not yet complete) and includes detailed descriptions of thousands of Plants in language that thrills me with its specificity and—for some lay readers like myself—opacity. For example, here is how the *Flora* describes the inflorescences (flowering parts) of Plants in Asteraceae, the Aster family:

> indeterminate heads (also called capitula); each head usually comprising a surrounding involucre of phyllaries (involucral bracts), a receptacle, and (1–)5–300+ florets; individual heads sessile or each borne on a peduncle; heads borne singly or in usually determinate, rarely indeterminate, arrays (cymiform, corymbiform, racemiform, spiciform, etc.); involucres sometimes subtended by calyculi (sing. calyculus); phyllaries borne in 1–5(–15+) series proximal to (i.e., outside of or abaxial to) the florets; receptacles usually flat to convex, sometimes conic or columnar, either paleate (bearing paleae or receptacular bracts that individually subtend some or all of the florets) or epaleate (lacking paleae); epaleate receptacles sometimes bristly or hairy or bearing subulate enations among the florets.

What Plants did these enslaved Ancestors have relationships with? What Plants could they have encountered as they practiced the forms of movement described in the advertisements? What Plants may have offered them food, medicine, shelter, beauty, company?

I started making lists of Plants that grow in the areas where the Ancestors "ran away." Some of these lists focused on Plants that could have been in flower at the time the Ancestor is reported to have "run away." Others focused on communities of Plants that have evolved to grow together in certain environments like swamps or sand dunes. Making these lists helped me feel protected as I engaged with this hard material. And it felt like a way of expressing gratitude and respect to the Ancestors, as well as to the Plants themselves. As I made the lists I often read the Plant names aloud, savoring their music.

"Benediction" is a collage of the time I've spent with these two archives. More introductory details are offered on pages 29-32.

❧

This book is traversed and inhabited by a music. Some signs of that music's presence appear in this book, like the tracks of an animal.

❧

How to use lyricism to investigate beauty in Black life, and Black dysfluent life, without romanticizing the experiences of the enslaved?

❧

Please feel free to read this book however you'd like. Front to back, back to front, tiddlywinking from page to page, slowly, quickly, not at all, forgotten at a friend's.

❧

Three quotes have guided me in this writing. They've helped me triangulate my location. The first comes from critic Hortense Spillers' book *Black, White, and in Color*. Reflecting on her 1987 essay "Mama's Baby, Papa's Maybe: An American Grammar Book," she writes:

> Slavery, as far as I am able to understand it, offers [a] . . . spectacle of successive
> displacements, in which case, nothing is what it appears to be, little or nothing is
> called by its name, precisely because the institutional order and its inhabitants on
> either side of the question (while the "sides" here are not moral equivalents) are
> trying, intolerably, to square a circle, or not to notice, like the Miltonic legions,

5

that they are trying to assure their oxygen supply of the social upside down; but the mandate [of "Mama's Baby, Papa's Maybe"] was to try to stand up this anarchically inverted arrangement of the social in order to hear its stutter more clearly.

The second quote comes from historian Eugene Genovese's book *Roll, Jordan, Roll*. He writes of the enslaved: "The stuttering, stammering, and downcast looks before white men betrayed not only fear but smoldering anger and resentment."

In "Benediction" I'm trying to follow Spillers's mandate to hear slavery's stutter (or slaveries' stutters—elsewhere Spillers writes that "there cannot have been a monolithic formation called 'slavery,' but, rather, several versions of slavery, both simultaneous and successive"). Here, as so often, I've tried to use music to try to hear. The musical notation in this book is only one layer of a bigger music, a long song I call on constantly to protect and guide me, and to undo my learning.

Genovese's statement strikes me as too knowing. In my experience, stuttering is too complex and opaque to be a matter of simply betraying fear, anger, resentment, or any other emotion. Here I've sought a different path in approaching the stutters that pass through the advertisements. I've tried to use my senses to attend to Plants, to music, to the Ancestors, and to the Stutter. I've tried to use this book as a musical instrument of unknowing.

❧

Is stuttering fugitive speech?

❧

Thank you, Chris Martin, for inviting me to write this book for Milkweed Editions' Multiverse series. Thank you, Hannah Emerson and Adam Wolfond, for your books—*The Kissing of Kissing* and *The Wanting Way*, respectively—the first two titles in this series. Thank you for inviting me to root further into the Stutter that my bodymind stewards.

The third quote comes from fiction writer Ursula Le Guin's book *Always Coming Home*:

The only way I can think to find them, the only archaeology that might be practical, is as follows: You take your child or grandchild in your arms, a young baby, not a year old yet, and go down into the wild oats in the field below the barn. Stand under the oak on the last slope of the hill, facing the creek. Stand quietly. Perhaps the baby will see something, or hear a voice, or speak to somebody there, somebody from home.

I.

OCTAGON OF WATER, MOVEMENT 2[*]

a channel crossing, two fruits
held in a rowboat.

The glottal block[†] becomes
a helmet for the spirit,
emblem of "perpetual
concealment,"[‡] a petal
trembling after a deer
leapt over it.

A grain of saxophone, ears
of green Wheat—we
divide and resow to reap
the sounds we found in dream.

Speech is porous to music.

What is the wound
reopening during the stutter?
How does it relate

---

[*] "Octagon of Water" is a long, ongoing poem. The first movement of the poem starts on page 89 of my book *The Clearing* with the line "Verbs await the oral," and ends on page 98 of that book with "speak of. All / ways emerge // like grace from / the Always, but / even the prom- / ise of com- / mon evening / Primrose must / move, must / metamorphose / like music into." I am grateful to you, Hannah Emerson, for teaching me about all ways and always.

[†] The kind of stutter I speak with is sometimes called a glottal block.

[‡] "We need those stubborn shadows where repetition leads to perpetual concealment, which is our form of resistance."—Édouard Glissant, *Caribbean Discourse*

to Morrison's flooding?* When
the Mississippi returns
to its former contours,
does the suture
we created by straightening
it open?

Dehiscence† is also

dissemination. The stutter
disperses silences, quiets,
small homes for listening—small
vocal fruit splitting.
There are 28,637 doors

in this music. The heart belongs
to the water. The ink belongs

to the wind, and when
lost syllables come home,
opening the wind
on the journey, when the water

arrives with mercy‡,

---

* "You know, they straightened out the Mississippi River in places, to make room for houses and livable acreage. Occasionally the river floods these places. 'Floods' is the word they use, but in fact it is not flooding; it is remembering. Remembering where it used to be. All water has a perfect memory and is forever trying to get back to where it was."—Toni Morrison, "The Site of Memory"

† Dehiscence refers to 1) when a wound reopens after being surgically sutured; 2) when the mature fruit, anther, or sporangium of a Plant splits to release seeds, pollen, or spores, respectively; 3) when the inner ear labyrinth is perforated, which can cause chronic vertigo and balance issues.

‡ Thank you, Delicia Daniels, for helping me hear this arrival.

when swallows
become one with
the waterfalls, and my mother
boils Cerasee tea for her soul,
what then?

PRAYER TO MY STUTTER #2

You restore
a living
shoreline
between word
and silence

The name of that silence is these Grasses in this wind, and the name of these Grasses in this wind is that other place on the other side of this instant. This instant is divided by curtains of water and the sound of shuddering time. A Sunflower reeling with sun, six hands stretched in offering. This unsearchable, uncancellable instant wraps the shoulders of the Grasses like a shawl stilled by the stoppage. White Pines whistle skyward. "With our beings shaped to songs of praise," writes the fifth-century theologian Pseudo-Dionysius. He continues: "What the scripture writers have to say regarding the divine names refers, in revealing praises, to the beneficent processions of God." What processes from the instant? Find the ceremony in every instant. "Every condition, movement, life, imagination, conjecture, name, discourse, thought, inception, being, rest, dwelling, unity, limit, infinity, the totality of existence," he writes, he sings. What is the name of this instant? *Where* is the name of this instant? Swimming in the Rappahannock, clinging to the swollen belly of that Ruby-throated Hummingbird.

"Bring anonymity," writes poet Tim Lilburn.

This morning come shyly or boldly into the fertile field, however you are, come, come and stay in the rearrangement, the pressure of thumb on Fescue blade, a year wheeling within a day, two round moments of warm mouth, finally at peace. The psalm is a key if only we can find the door. Do not swallow your dysfluent voice. Let it erupt in its volcanic flowering. Stoppage

thence passage, aporia, Poppy bursting with fragrant seed.

PRAYER TO MY STUTTER #4

You help me
caress the Asters I am
learning to trust
you as one
trusts
a sturdy ladder
climbing
into still air

PRAYER TO MY STUTTER #6

The syllable's left hand encountered the depths, fell slow through the listening.
The syllable told me to refuse it, to pour it back into itself.

A sound of fire rising into day: a sound of water withdrawing into sound.
Every word is an answer, every answer an arrow, every arrow a river, every river a word.

I belong to you. You let the eagles lead me to the mountain in the music, the mountain of
winter, the mountain that is home.

Be still and let the fountain fill with patience.

OCTAGON OF WATER, MOVEMENT 4

i
Stutters and Asters
are sisters, clerestory
to a space of ceremony.
Their syntaxes similar,
pink instruments ready
in the still air.

ii
Early spring in Norfolk, Virginia:
my best friend Luísa
and I pass a Tree:
Redbud (*Cercis canadensis*).
The Tree has flowers but no leaves yet.

She teaches me a word
for when a Tree does this:
hysteranthy.

Is a stutter a form of early
music?

II.

LITURGY OF THE NAME

What are the repercussions for your spirit when we steal your name?
Or, what are the repercussions of your name being inseparable from a certain silence?

The curtain of the syllable

"What's your name?" This question has made me afraid my whole life. But over the years, after thousands of glottal blocks on my name, I've been led to a grove of unknowing. What *is* my name? How should I spell it? Did I consent to be baptized? Were those baptismal waters dysfluent? Does my name preserve this perfect dysfluency? I skip the crack in the sidewalk. I slip out the back door of time. Strip me of my name, all my mothers and fathers, forever. Lead me to the threshold of the curtained aperture. Douse me with perfume. Abyss on both sides—

We've been trying to tell you for so long. We finally sent the deer to tell you, hoping you'd listen to them. They leapt past you and everyone else, scalded by moonlight. Go see where they drink! Follow them. Bring your needle and thread, your mascara and blush. You'll try your hardest not to lose them, but you still will.

We invented patience. Go see where they drink. What color are their tongues? Do you fear illusions?

I cannot hear them.

If we fashion a new silence for you to wear on your breast, will that help? The brook is crooked. Drop this book into it once you've learned these words by heart. Hurry, slowly. Go see where they think.

Perpetual ardor

What might a baptismal melisma* sound like? Or a melismatic baptism? A page illuminated by a melismatic lamp.

---

* Melisma refers to when a singer sings more than one note per syllable. For an example, see the syllables "Oh, oh" in the sheet music in *Benediction*. See also Aretha Franklin's performance of "Amazing Grace" on her 1972 album *Amazing Grace*.

A bestiary of silences

A pane of water separates me from my name.
Silence for me has always been as feral and divine as animals. I encounter certain species of silence through stutter and through music.

The song of union: underlying the song is water, underlying the water is breath, underlying the breath is the roar. I sing of distance. I try and fail to see through the waterfall and in the act of trying and failing over and over I release into something. I carve my name into the glass.

When someone asks you your name, we take your name as an offering.

When someone asks you your name, we come out of your mouth first.

When someone asks you your name, we flood your vocal tract with silence. The silence usually lasts between five and ten seconds, but can be upwards of thirty. What is the nature of that silence, between when you're asked your name and when we permit you to utter it? Your body is our vessel. In that interval you have no name, and your essence is brought into question and relief.

This is all invisible to the person who asked you your name. It is not for them to see.

Often you anticipate the absent name. You dread it. You walk toward someone you know you'll have to introduce yourself to. You shudder in eros. The asphyxia we give you conceals another breath, stolen from the task of uttering your name and assigned to this ulterior, interior scene. That stolen breath starts a movement in another

direction.

Time

dilates.

Sometimes people laugh and say, "Did you forget your name?" How far down does this question go?

Layers of silver light tilt over a canyon in my spirit like cirrus.

Here I am, father, tilted toward you in all my—

If I continue to tilt, within the interval of stuttering on my name, I fall further into the abyss and toward the center.

Hesitation creates distance. I revolve around my name: a tower with a moat of silence. My name determines the length of my passage on those waters, my voice a ferry, a new wind blowing.

In "The Name of God and the Linguistic Theory of the Kabbalah," philosopher Gershom Sholem traces how the name of God in Jewish tradition became ineffable: "The most significant moment in this development and at the same time the most paradoxical moment is the fact that the name, by which God calls himself and which is used to utter invocations, withdraws from the acoustic sphere and becomes unpronounceable. To begin with it is tolerated for a few especially rare occasions within the temple as a word which may be pronounced, for example when the priest gives the blessing or on the Day of Atonement (Yom Kippur); after this, however, and above all after the destruction of the temple, it was completely withdrawn into the realm of the ineffable."

My name, in the time when I cannot utter it, maps the space within me. In an instant the Stutter shuttles me from the present—the barber just asked me my name, my voice fluttering in my throat, struggling not to tremble as the razor presses on my temples—to an ancient place of breath, name, silence, time, creation.

The Stutter hides my name not just from the person I'm speaking to, but from myself. The Kabbalists describe "letters of concealment" which are used to form a name which conceals the true Name of God.

Whenever I approach a moment when I may need to introduce myself, a liturgy begins. I'm in line at Shake Shack and I know the cashier will ask for my name once I've ordered my hamburger. The liturgy begins in line, my spirit already inhaling the incense of anticipation. How do I prepare? A vector of attention and tension stretches out within me like a taut violin string ready to vibrate.

For the past five years I've been setting the following text to music, to different melodies:

quaemadmodum desiderat cervus ad fontes aquarum ita desiderat anima mea ad te deus. As the stag desires the streams of water, so my soul desires you, o god. The text comes from St. Jerome's Latin Vulgate translation of Psalm 42, verse 2 in the Tanakh (also known as the Hebrew Bible). I love the way this verse encompasses wild animals, desire, thirst, water, and god: all things that help me understand my stutter.

When the door of my vocal cords closes, another opens. And through that open door I escape into a region I do not know what to call but which is vaster than the space of my body. You could say: my name is the door to my being, and in that interval when I'm stuttering, the door is left wide open and my being rushes out. What rushes in?

When I was growing up, my mother told me to repeat certain verses from the Tanakh in order to "heal" my stutter. One of those verses was the second half of Isaiah 32:4: "the tongue of the stammerers shall be ready to speak plainly." I said it over and over, sometimes while looking at myself in the mirror, in desperation.

In setting Jerome's verse to music, have I been furnishing music for a ceremony?

My stutter is a form of thirst, a calling in the throat, a seeking after the only thing that will quench me: sound, thunder, god.

When I sit down to play or sing this music, water passes before my eyes. I stare into the distance and the water guides me further.

A slowly spinning diamond in the winter sun.

I put on my suit of water. Turquoise, aquamarine.

The ceremony can begin as early as when I decide to go to Shake Shack; I'll be there in about thirty minutes[*]. I've already begun this process of washing myself, changing my garment, preparing to undergo once again the Liturgy of the Name.

---

[*] Thank you, Maria Stuart, for teaching me about this ceremony.

III.

ABOUT THE BENEDICTION

"Benediction" is an ongoing hymn. Three movements of the hymn are offered in the following pages (two in Part III and one in Part V). The word *benediction* comes from Latin *bene dicere*: "to speak well."

The hymn focuses solely on "runaway slave" advertisements (see this book's introduction for more information) concerning Ancestors who are described as Negro or Mulatto. Further, the hymn focuses on Ancestors who are described as stuttering, stammering, or having speech impediments or "stoppages" in their speech.

I look to these advertisements as an archive of Black dysfluency.

⚘

Could Black dysfluency be a form of ancestral wisdom?

⚘

From this point on in the book, I will refer to and address Plants as Elders*. The names of the Plant Elders appear in purple throughout this book†.

The more I live with my stutter, with the Stutter that I steward in my body, the more I feel and know, or unknow, that this stutter is no less a part of the earth than the rest of my body. This stutter has come from the land and the water. It knows the Plant Elders, and there is much I can learn, and have learned, about my stutter by spending time with these Elders. Names run through the Grasses, and when I stutter on my name, I am brought into the field.

---

* Not to be confused with Plants who have the word *elder* in their name! For example, I refer to the Plant *Sambucus canadensis* as Elder Elderberry, and *Acer negundo* as Elder Box Elder.

† Thank you, Adam Wolfond, for inviting me to use color in this book.

The hymn sings to different Plant Elders that are native and naturalized to the areas where the Ancestors lived. Further, the hymn speculates about moments of connection the Ancestors may have experienced with these Plant Elders while they "ran away."

As described in the introduction to this book, I composed fragments of text by rearranging words that appear in the relevant advertisement (following poet m. nourbeSe philip's method in the book *Zong!*). These fragments appear in italics in "Benediction." (Latin names for Plant Elders also appear in italics.) Sometimes I use parts of words (e.g. "Negro" in the advertisement becomes "gro" in the fragment; "master" becomes "Aster"). I've retained capitalization (e.g. Creek, Dwelling, etc.) and spelling (e.g. callico, cloathing, etc.) as they appear in the ads (except for Plant Elders, whose names I capitalize).

Movement 2 responds to an ad concerning an Ancestor named Betsey. Betsey is reported to have "run away" from Charleston, South Carolina in the United States. But instead of restricting myself to the single ad, for eight days straight I chose one ad a day from the same newspaper issue, thus expanding the number of words available to compose the fragments. Some of these additional ads were placed by people who had lost objects—a "Pocket Book, containing a number of papers"; an "UMBRELLA, which is covered in green silk." Others announce land ("a valuable Tide Swamp Plantation on Pedee river") or goods ("one grand PIANO") for sale. These ads betray some of the ways Black people have been considered akin to objects and "denied the capacity to claim normative personhood," as poet and critic Fred Moten reminds.*

In Movement 2, the fragments themselves are set to music. Some of these fragments also appear in Movement 1. I refer to Movement 2 as "Octave," evoking the musical meaning of the word, as well as the practice, in some forms of Christianity, of commemorating a saint for eight days straight.

"Octave" is anchored in a list of Plants that grow in and around Charleston. Each Plant name is preceded by a form of address: "we revere you," "we listen to you," "we love you," etc. Months after slowly compiling the list, I decided to read it aloud and note which syllables I stuttered on, and for how long I stuttered. Over the course of a few weeks, I read it aloud to Luísa, my friend and editor Chris, and my friend and collaborator James. At the end of one of these reading sessions, Chris asked if I had read it to the Yellow-Crowned Night Herons

---

* Thank you, heidi andrea restrepo rhodes, for helping me think about objecthood and Blackness.

(*Nyctanassa violacea*) I often see fishing in a marsh near Luísa's and my home in Norfolk, Virginia. I said no, but that I would try the following morning.

I read the final names in "Octave" to a Yellow-Crowned Night Heron I saw walking on a stone wall along The Hague, a waterway in Norfolk. They disappeared into a stand of *Iva frutesceens*, Elder Marsh Elder. I kept reading and walking in the direction the Heron had gone. A few minutes later, a Heron appeared from the Plants, maybe the same Heron, maybe not.

❧

In her poem "Testimony Stoops to Mother Tongue," m. nourbeSe philip writes: "in my mother's mouth / shall I / use / the father's tongue." Like many members of the African diaspora, I don't know what languages my African ancestors spoke before the middle passage. I have my father tongue—English—but what are my mother tongues?

Could the Stutter that passes through my body be one of those mother tongues? The Stutter—older than English, maybe older than any language, maybe older than speech itself?

In this text, I've addressed the Plant Elders with English and Latin names only. I want to call them by their Indigenous names (especially for North American Plant Elders), but I don't speak any Indigenous languages, nor do I feel I have permission to use those names here. I don't have relationships with any Indigenous keepers of Plant knowledge. I want to respect the keepers of this knowledge. Scientists Nikki Bass and Robin Wall Kimmerer have taught me a lot in relation to this and many other questions.

❧

The [bracketed] text that appears later in this section is a score for and transcription of music. Music is also represented with staff lines.

No worries if you don't read music. The audiobook with music is available at milkweed.org and wherever audiobooks are sold.

For simplicity, the sheet music is all in the key of C major. The singer is free to transpose the music to whichever key and octave feels best.

The music is notated without meter. The only rhythmic information notated is a difference between shorter notes ● and longer notes ◐. The singer is free to sing in any rhythm they desire. The way I sing this music on the audiobook is just one interpretation of the rhythm.

Rests ∤, which indicate that the musician should be silent for a specified amount of time, appear in Movement 2.

A bird's eye ⌢, which indicates that the musician should hold the note for a longer amount of time, appears in Movement 3.

❀

Frances. John Smart. Lucy. Harry. Mariah. Bob. Paro. Nanny. Adam. Fanny. John Carr. Rose. Hannah. Betsey. Neptune:

What names did they call themselves? Because it was common practice for enslavers to name or rename the enslaved, I don't know how these Ancestors felt about the names they're called in the ads. I honor each Ancestor's relationship to names and naming.

What pronouns did they use? In this book I refer to these Ancestors using she/her and he/him pronouns. These are the pronouns used in the advertisements. I recognize that I don't know how these Ancestors related to their gender. I honor each Ancestor's relationship to pronouns and gender.

Advertisements concerning these Ancestors form the source material for "Benediction." Quotations from these advertisements appear in quotation marks in the hymn (e.g. "stammers a little").

Gratitude to these Ancestors for their speech, their breath, their lives.

❀

"Now unto him who is able to keep us from falling . . ." With these words from the Epistle of Jude in the New Testament, my Jamaican maternal grandfather would begin the Benediction Prayer that ended Sunday morning service at his church in Brooklyn, New York. His Black Baptist and Pentecostal cadences have always been models for me of a speech porous to music.

BENEDICTION, MOVEMENT 1

The choir chants:

where is the prose   *that will house our rigour*

where is the prose   *that will house our stoppage*

where is the prose   *that will house our living*

where is the prose   *that will house our cloathing*

What name did Ancestor Lucy call herself? We do not know. We honor her relationship to her own name.

According to the advertisement, she "ran away" on March 19, 1797, on or near land and water traditionally stewarded by, among others, the Sewee people—also known as Charleston, South Carolina.

We honor the holiness of her speech, and of her whole being.

We thank all the Plant Elders for creating the oxygen she breathed.

the stutters may endeavour
to return
to the Creek

stutters born   *before April was born*

stutters may be before speaks
may may be before April
return may be before quest

our Reward is being
*in quest of stutters**

is the stutter an arbour
of maybe

---

*   Thank you, James Harrison Monaco, for helping me hear this.

the arbour of maybe made I into our

[The drip comes out

onto the porch of melisma,

in the sun on a new morning.]

the art of the stutter is to give away
being
on time

the art of the stutter
is to utter in time
*not on time**

[Tonal sleep—two drop perhaps
underswimming.]

---

* I am so grateful to you, Iya Milta Vega Cardona, for teaching me about being in time.

"stammers a little."

[Therefore, the plumb line

hanging from jay wing]

[swings through   ~~syllable~~

clouds of syllable.]

[A shred of gnawed knowing.]

What name did Ancestor Bob call himself? We do not know. We honor his relationship to his own name.

According to the ad, he "ran away" on April 8, 1786, likely on or near land and water traditionally stewarded by, among others, the Sewee and Santee peoples—also known as Berkeley County, South Carolina.

We honor the holiness of his speech, and of his whole being.

We thank all the Plant Elders for creating the oxygen he breathed.

is that speech impediment a black chant
offered by the water side

[What the sound is]
[is]
[is]
[is]
[is the sound of some]
[of the things happening in the soil.]

black information is information about passage

dock above water
name above forehead

What name did Ancestor Hannah call herself? We do not know. We honor her relationship to her own name.

According to the advertisement, she "ran away" on October 4, 1823, likely on or near land and water traditionally stewarded by, among others, the Sewee people—also known as Charleston, South Carolina.

We honor the holiness of her speech, and of her whole being.

We thank all the Plant Elders for creating the oxygen she breathed.

What name did Ancestor Harry call himself? We do not know. We honor his relationship to his own name.

According to the ad, he "ran away" on January 14, 1759, on or near land and water traditionally stewarded by, among others, the Munsee Lenape people—also known as Staten Island, New York.

We honor the holiness of his speech, and of his whole being.

We thank all the Plant Elders for creating the oxygen he breathed.

a river of years has crossed

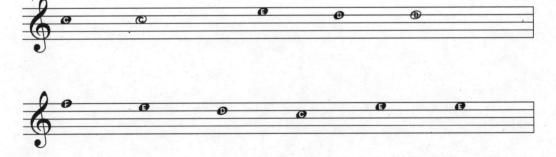

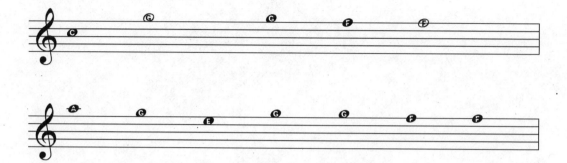

the instant

Elder Yarrow (*Achillea millefolium*)

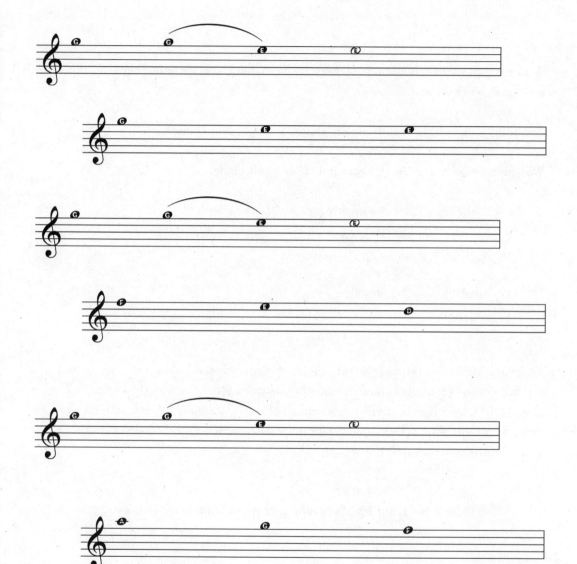

We speak with an Aster

What name did Ancestor Frances call herself? We do not know. We honor her relationship to her own name.

According to the ad, she "ran away" on January 22, 1750, near London.

We honor the holiness of her speech, and of her whole being.

We thank all the Plant Elders for creating the oxygen she breathed.

[hold my hair aside in horse hours]

[The name shall bring] [back] [years] [when it returns silver, astride a chestnut] [mare,] [astride a story of gossamer] [and fireshouting, astride a solitary aster], [free from] [free.] [Held, held.] [Here, anonymous annuals blossom] [lessons.] [Here, antiphonal politics hold up traffic.] [Here, a dehiscing question honors the incarcerated.] [Here, ceramics make quiet circles. Hold] [up]

Elder Mosses, did any of you offer yourselves as a pillow? Thank you.

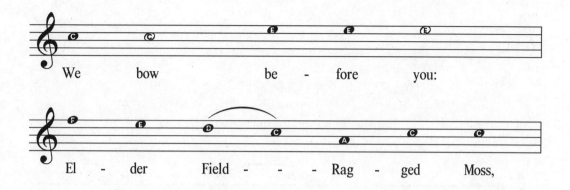

with a speech Impediment, the Instant can flower

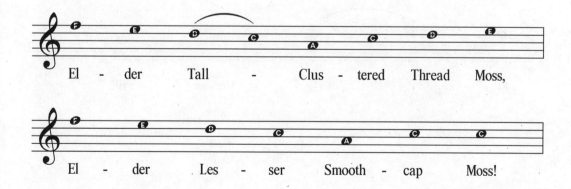

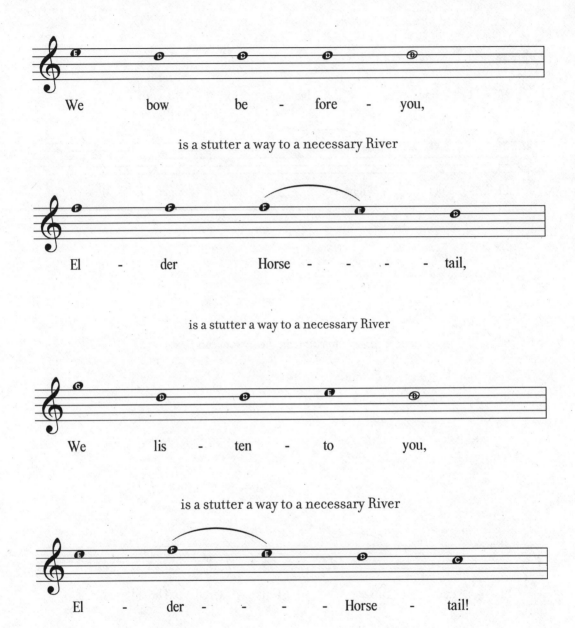

[raiment]

[drape]

[drape]

"sometimes stutters a little"

[raiment]

[raiment   ]

[drape]   [raiment]

[drape]

What name did Ancestor Rose call herself? We do not know. We honor her relationship to her own name.

According to the ad, she "ran away" on September 16, 1780, likely on or near land and water traditionally stewarded by, among others, the Munsee Lenape people—also known as Manhattan, New York.

We honor the holiness of her speech, and of her whole being.

We thank all the Plant Elders for creating the oxygen she breathed.

there is no name more fertile

names sealed up in the approaching season

the name of the approaching season will be written on the river
the instant he stutters on Rose
the Rose will cut a window

they LOST their UMBRELLA to the swamp

no person will harness stutters

What name did Ancestor Paro call himself? We do not know. We honor his relationship to his own name.

According to the ad, he "ran away" on May 4, 1796, on or near land and water traditionally stewarded by, among others, the Sewee and Santee peoples—also known as Berkeley County, South Carolina.

We honor the holiness of his speech, and of his whole being.

We thank all the Plant Elders for creating the oxygen he breathed.

Did you pass through a Woodland Community that includes: Elder Longleaf Pine (*Pinus palustris*) in the overstory; Elder Summersweet (*Clethra alnifolia*), Elder Blue Huckleberry (*Gaylussacia frondosa*), and Elder Running Oak (*Quercus pumila*) in the woody understory; and Elder Little Bluestem (Schizachyrium scoparium) in the layer closest to the ground? As far as is known, this type of Plant Community is unique to the Coastal Plain of South Carolina, and is critically imperiled.

when shall the name of the morning be received

Did you pass through a Swamp Woodland Community that includes: Elder Pond Cypress (*Taxodium ascendens*) in the overstory; Elder Swamp Holly (*Ilex amelanchier*) and Elder Titi (*Cyrilla racemiflora*) in the shrub layer; and Elder Virginia Chainfern (*Woodwardia virginica*) in the layer closest to the ground?

"stutters when spoken to"

We bow be - fore you: El - der Long - leaf Pine,

crown them with stammers

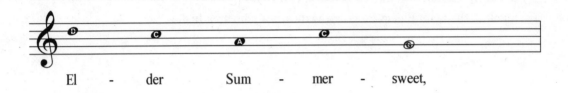

El - der Sum - mer - sweet,

and crown them with away

El - der Lit - tle Blue - stem, -

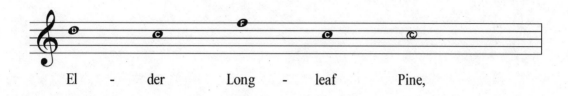

El - der Long - leaf Pine,

morning alone in morning
a small tuft of light

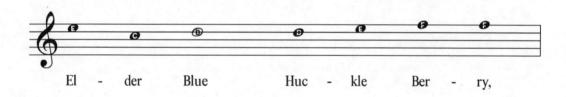

El - der Blue Huc - kle Ber - ry,

speech shall long for stammers

stammers shall long for something older

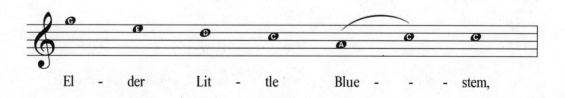

El - der Lit - tle Blue - - stem,

55

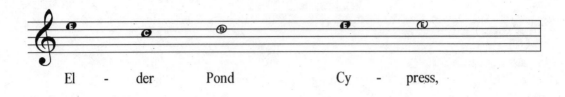

El   -   der   Pond   Cy   -   press,

is being black sufficient proof of being

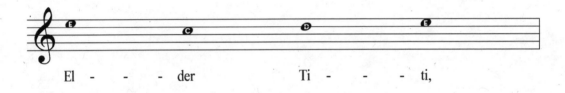

El - - - der   Ti - - - ti,

if being is going over a long Bridge
what has been carried to the end of the Bridge

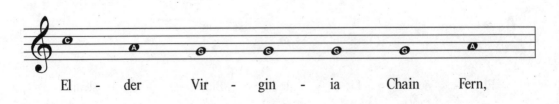

El - der   Vir - gin - ia   Chain   Fern,

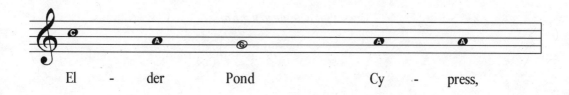

El - der Pond Cy - press,

can the project of the stammers be perceived

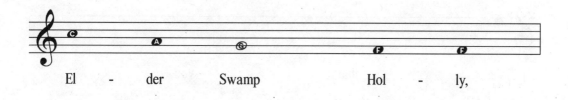

El - der Swamp Hol - ly,

morning is something years long

El - der Vir - gin - ia Chain Fern!

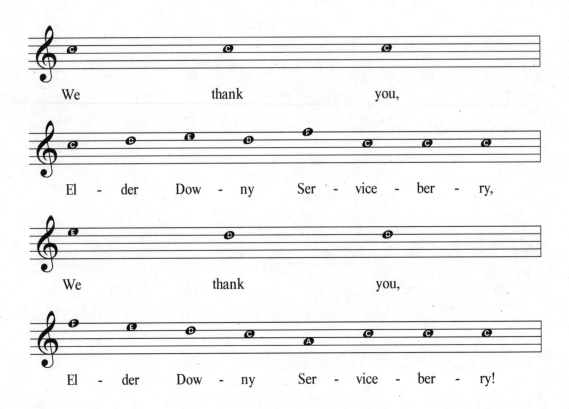

We thank you,

El - der Dow - ny Ser - vice - ber - ry,

We thank you,

El - der Dow - ny Ser - vice - ber - ry!

Trust that, with time, that name will be an arbor

"Runaways" might change their names to protect themselves.

are stutters vessels full of winter
are stutters chosen
are stutters empty bottles

close
the window
of the well

Did you touch, smell, see any white Elder Downy Serviceberry (*Amelanchier arborea*) blossoms on your journey? Did you hear or see any Ruby-throated Hummingbirds (Archilochus colubris) nectaring at the blossoms, flying north from their wintering grounds thousands of miles away?

[between sepal and petal lies a soft sound folded
like a pearl learning contour]

[can names be deciduous]

What name did Ancestor Nanny call herself? We do not know. We honor her relationship to her own name.

According to the ad, she "ran away" on May 28, 1814, likely on or near land and water traditionally stewarded by, among others, the Powhatan Confederacy—also known as Richmond, Virginia.

We honor the holiness of her speech, and of her whole being.

We thank all the Plant Elders for creating the oxygen she breathed.

According to the ads, Ancestor Lucy "ran away" more than once. Another ad was placed on September 10, 1794, but it does not give the date when she "ran away."

We honor the holiness of her speech, and of her whole being.

We thank all the Plant Elders for creating the oxygen she breathed.

Elder Longleaf Pine (*Pinus palustris*)

the black scribe shall NOTICE
the aria

are questions empty
bottles with a name
written inside

the stutters shall deliver years
of stolen time

What name did Ancestor John Carr call himself? We do not know. We honor his relationship to his own name.

According to the ad, on August 4, 1769 he "ran away" from a ship docked at Shadwell Basin on the river Thames in London. The ship had arrived that day from St. Kitts.

We honor the holiness of his speech, and of his whole being.

We thank all the Plant Elders for creating the oxygen he breathed.

[hummed theft in the space of calling]

"stammer[ed] . . . when questioned."

her name is covered with green
silk inside green
glass

The ad says you played French horn and violin. Did your instruments bring you joy? Did you carry them with you? If so, how did you protect them? Did you encounter Elder Bracken Fern (*Pteridium aquilinum*), with their fiddlehead fronds tucked under the snow? Did you stuff your clothes with their dry fronds to stay warm?

[crying as first skill, then tuned sky
like deerskin transfigured drum]

stutters MARK TONGUES
and paper

to have a name is to be asked questions
about a name

to receive a name is to close a window

to have a name is to have LOST
the time of no name

Did you hide in any prickly thickets of Elder Blackthorn (*Prunus spinosa*) or Elder Hawthorn (*Crataegus monogyna*)?*

---

*   Thank you, Paul Aston, for teaching me about these Plants Elders.

We   kneel   be - fore - - - you,

the stutters will be harbours
for years

❦

stutters: a false offence

❦

the name shall bring back years when it returns

❦

they play the stutter
as a violin

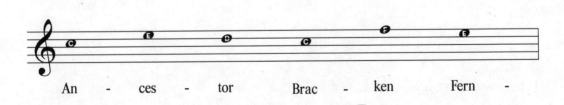

An - ces - tor   Brac - ken   Fern -

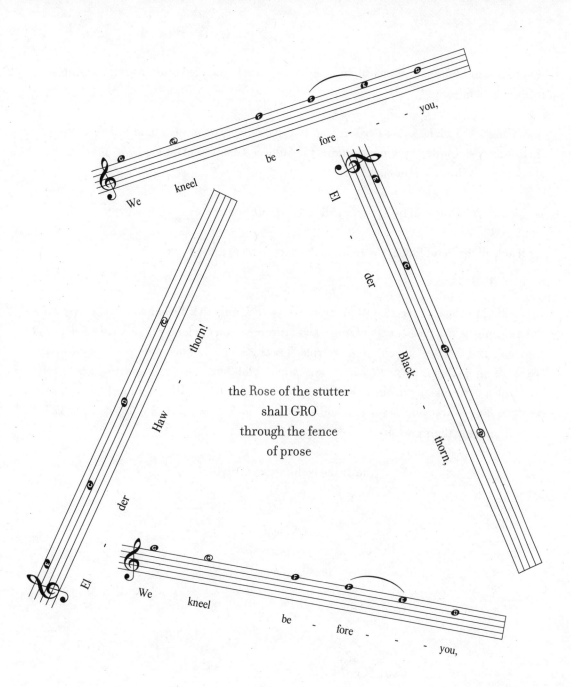

What name did Ancestor Adam call himself? We do not know. We honor his relationship to his own name.

According to the ad, he "ran away" on August 4, 1782, likely on or near land and water traditionally stewarded by, among others, the Munsee Lenape and Canarsie peoples—also known as Queens, New York.

We honor the holiness of his speech, and of his whole being.

We thank all the Plant Elders for creating the oxygen he breathed.

Let us sing to some of the Plant Elders in the Aster family that flower in August—and have done so long before the concept of August was invented—on the land you may have journeyed through*. Did you see, touch, smell purple flowers: Elder Smooth Aster (*Symphyotrichum laeve*)? White: Elder Yarrow (*Achillea millefolium*) and Elder Pearly Everlasting (*Anaphalis margaritacea*)? Pinkish purple: Elder Field Thistle (*Cirsium discolor*)? Yellow: Elder Spanish Needles (*Bidens bipinnata*)? Pinkish white: Elder Climbing Hempweed (*Mikania scandens*)? Did you smile in their presence?

[the drone is the space of crying]

[*much obliged*
to winter
the size of paper]

---

*   Thank you, Luísa, for the reminder!

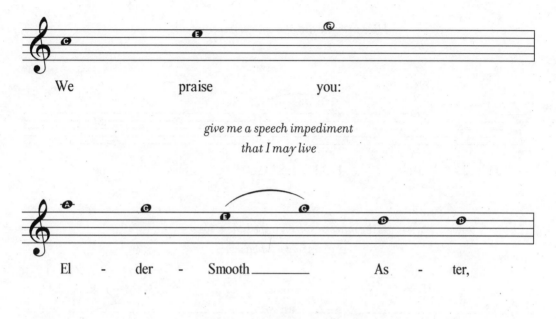

We   praise   you:

give me a speech impediment
that I may live

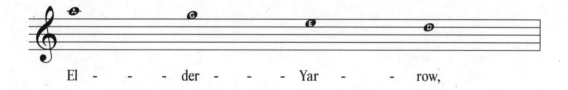

El – der – Smooth _____   As – ter,

give me a speech impediment
that I may give
notice

El – – – der – – – Yar – – row,

give me a speech impediment
that I may notice
Asters

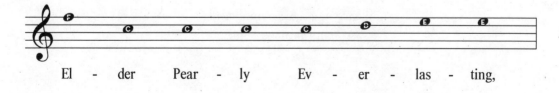

El – der   Pear – ly   Ev – er – las – ting,

I live with the aid of a speech impediment

is the office of speech impediment to carry
years in a gold basket

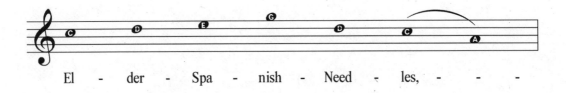

is the cure to gro Asters

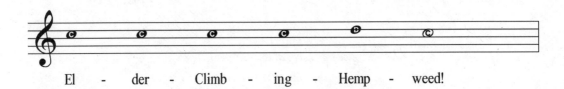

give me a speech impediment
that I may be a scribe
for Asters

Did you see a Small Copper Butterfly (Lycaena phlaeas) fluttering toward Elder Yarrow for nectar?

What name did Ancestor Fanny call herself? We do not know. We honor her relationship to her own name.

According to the ad, she "ran away" on June 7, 1855, likely on or near land and water traditionally stewarded by, among others, the Lumbee people—also known as Cumberland County, North Carolina.

We honor the holiness of her speech, and of her whole being.

We thank all the Plant Elders for creating the oxygen she breathed.

For centuries Swamp Plant Communities have sheltered people escaping enslavement. Did you pass through a Swamp Community that includes: Elder Cherrybark Oak (*Quercus pagoda*) and Elder Green Ash (*Fraxinus pennsylvanica*) in the overstory; Elder Florida Maple (*Acer floridanum*) and Elder Ironwood (*Carpinus caroliniana*) in the shrub layer; and Elder River Oats (*Chasmanthium latifolium*) and Elder Eastern Star Sedge (*Carex radiata*) in the layer closest to the ground?

the morning will deliver her evening name and the evening will deliver her morning name

carrying morning on their TONGUES

they will dispose of their name on the most reasonable terms
and her time will be paid in full

We praise＿＿ you: El - der Cher - ry - bark Oak,

my impediment will be

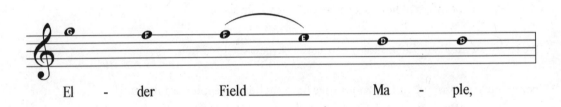

El - der Field＿＿＿＿＿ Ma - ple,

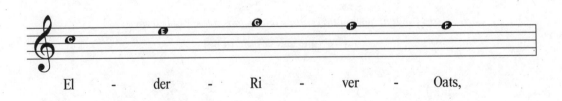

El - der - Ri - ver - Oats,

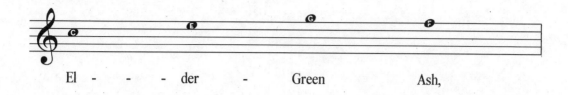

El - - - der - Green Ash,

my Dwelling

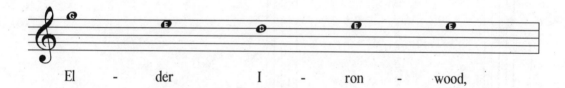

El - der I - ron - wood,

[seek ways to still the music and show the powder]

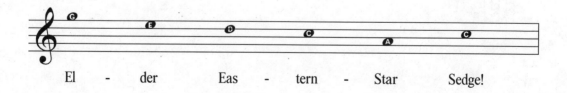

El - der Eas - tern - Star Sedge!

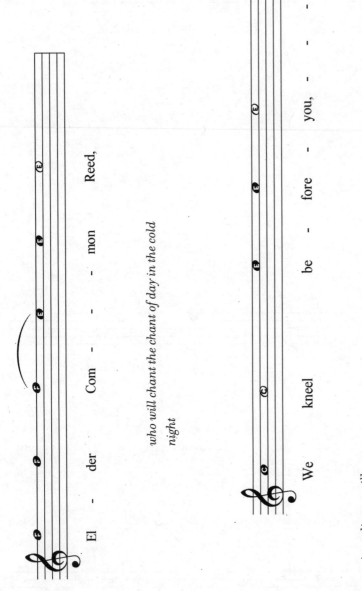

El - der   Com -   -   mon   Reed,

who will chant the chant of day in the cold

night

We   kneel   be   -   fore   -   you,   -   -   -

impediment will water
the fields of speech

[the music listens when we forget: to itself, to the land and the water,
to the sky] [and] [to the pressure]

Elder Blackthorn (*Prunus spinosa*)

According to another ad, Ancestor Paro "ran away" again on July 5, 1796, likely on or near land and water traditionally stewarded by, among others, the Sewee and Santee peoples—also known as Berkeley County, South Carolina.

Did you encounter Elder Cattail (*Typha latifolia*) growing by the marsh? Scientist Robin Wall Kimmerer teaches about the many gifts Elder Cattail offers us. They produce a gel between the bases of their leaves that is cooling and antimicrobial, a powerful protectant for skin exposed to a lot of sun.

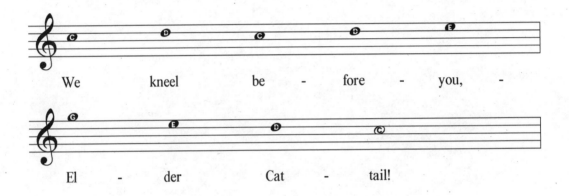

We   kneel   be   -   fore   -   you,   -

El   -   der   Cat   -   tail!

Their leaf bases are also coated with white cells called aerenchyma that add cushioning and make the leaves perfect for a sleeping mat.

The ad says you were "an excellent cook" and that "Masters of vessels are particularly requested to beware carrying him off," as you may have found employment as a cook aboard a ship. Did you roast any of Elder Cattail's rhizomes, or soak them in water to make porridge?

[all the names of winter
are sealed up in the kernel
of the instant]

evening of no

they questioned all they carried
they carried all they finished
they finished all they expected
they did not expect all that called them
they named all they questioned
they are separate from all that speaks well
they carried all they questioned

there are no TONGUES more fertile
than TONGUES with

the October river questions any person or persons willing to receive questions

their letters are not instant

sutters know a river that letters do not know

above the river of either or is a library
of carrying

advance low and empty, close to the morning
know different streets

Did she stay with her two daughters or her mother? How did they care for her?

What name did your mother call you?

the stutters will have repaired time
please notice the Winter sealed up in their stutters

a library of empty vessels and full vessels
she has her UMBRELLA for when the years fall

On March 19, 2022, we gathered at the Haw River in North Carolina, on land and water that has been stewarded by, among others, the Catawba people. We gathered to remember you, Ancestor Mariah. We stood in a loose circle and held the lineaments of a ceremony. Courtney and Tamika offered honey and flowers to Oshun. Luísa identified a stand of Elder Horsetail (*Equisetum* sp.) living next to where we stood.

According to the ad, you "ran away" on March 24, 1828, likely near the "Haw River, near Murphey's Mill."

Months later, I invited everyone to offer a word for you, for the ceremony:

Alexis: Star

Chris: Snake

Courtney: Sovereignty

JJJJJerome: Sky

Luísa: Sacrament

Sharon: Sweetness

Tamika: Visceral

[the clay encyclopedia] [hiding] [a third] [kind] [of listening]

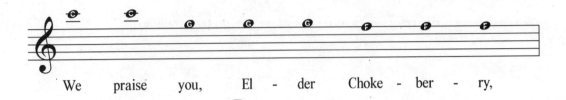

We   praise   you,   El – der   Choke – ber – ry,

is impediment a R U N
in red silk

or a ROSE
in an instant
of green

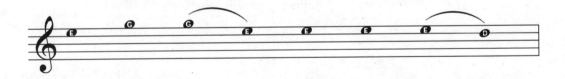

the callico
the sattin
the silk

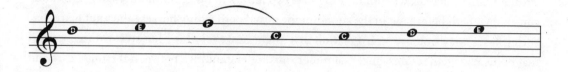

speech impediment brings green
into speech

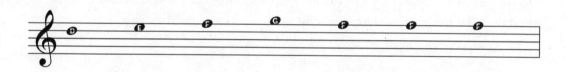

my speech impediment brings me to the the
and to the all

[I went out early. The horses at the center of my heart. A purple Rose hanging behind, fire not yet dead, never shall die, within, core, I went out past the Apricot orchards, needing the dark, writing nothing, having written nothing save two letters to my grandmothers, one alive, one gone home, both before me in the center of my heart, both riding horses, chestnut mare, bay sorrel, years away from any conversation that might heal everything but still within the pearl that holds us together. Messenger, summer, misunderstandings between the one heart and the other heart, dawn already touching our arms.

I went out earlier the next morning, hurting, holding a dented lantern, needing acupuncture but afraid to admit it. Reading as I walked, my grandmothers at my left and right sides, conversing dryly and simply as bread. Rising envelope of rain perfume, all alabasters, shuddering alive, years of doubt waiting for an alchemy, a hearing, the whole Apricot orchard untouched by greed.

Grandmothers, please hold me in the green as long as possible, though I may scratch to leave. You know what is best for me. Learn me into new wandering. Cannot hold on until evening. We spent the late morning tying the canes of the Climbing Rose to the iron fence.]

no Book
all stutters

Elder Chokeberry (*Aronia arbuitfolia*)

"The proper name of God is a list."—Valentina Izmirlieva

BENEDICTION, MOVEMENT 2 (OCTAVE)

The choir chants:

wwwwwwwwwwwwwwwwwwwwwwwwwwwwwwwwwwwwwwwwWe bbbbbbbbbbbbbbbbbbbbb bbbbb bbbbbbbbbbbbbbbbbbbbbbbbbbbbbbbbbbbbbbbbbbbbbbbbbbbbbbbbbbbbbbbbbb bbbbbbbbbb bbbbbbbbbbbbbbbbbbbbbbbbbbbbbbbbbbbbbelong to you, Elder New Jersey Tea (*Ceanothus aa aaaaaaaaaaaaaaaaaaaaaaaaaaaaaaaaaaaaaaaaaaaaaaamericanus*) * We revere you, Elder bbbb bbbbbbbbbbbbbbbbbbbbbbbbbbbbbbbbbbbbbbbbbbbbbbBig Cordgrass (*Spartina cynosuroides*) * We praise you, Elder Late-flowering bbbbbbbbbbbbbbbbbbbbbbbbbbbbbbbbbbbbbbbbbbbbbbbb bbbbbbbbbbbbbbbbbbbbbbbbbbbbbbbbbbbbbbbbbbbbbbbbbbbbbbbbbbbbbbbbbbbbbbbbbbbbbbbb bbbbbBoneset (*Eupatorium serotinum*) * We worship you, Elder Netted Nutrush (*Scleria rrrrrr rrrrrrrrrrrrrrrrrrrrrrrrrrrrrreticularis*) * We bow before you, Elder Deerberry (*Vaccinium stamineum*) * We listen to you, Elder Gallberry (*Ilex cccccccccccccccccccccccccccccccccccccccccccccccccccccccc ccccccccccccccccccccccoriacea*) * We need you, Elder ddddddddddddddddddddddddddddddddddd ddddddddddddddddddddddddddddddddddddddddddddddddddddddddddddddddddddddddddddddd dddddddddddddddddddddddddddddddddddddddddddddddddddddddddddddddddddDowny Goldenrod (*Solidago ppppppppppppppppppppppppppppppppppppppppppppppppppppppppppppppppppppppppp ppppppppppppppppppppppppppppppppppppppppppppppppppppppppppetiolaris*) * We kneel before you, Elder Goat's Rue (*Tephrosia virginiana*) * We worship you, Elder Blue-joint ppppppppppppppppppppp pppppppppppppppppppppppppppppppppppppppppppppppppppppppppppppppppppppppppppppppp ppppppppppppppppppppppppppppppppppppppppppppppppppppppppppppppppppppppppppppppppp pppppppppppppppppppppppppppppppppPanic Grass (*Panicum ttttttttttttttttttttttttttttttttttt ttttttttttttttttttttttttttttttttttttttttttttttttttttttttttttttttttttttttenerum*) * We revere you, Elder Beaked pppppppppppppppppppppppppppppppppppppppppppppppppppppppppppppppppppppppppppppppp ppppppPanic Grass (*Panicum anceps*) * We venerate you, Elder Maryland Meadow Beauty (*Rhexia mariana*) * We kneel before you, Elder Summer Grape (*Vitis aeaeaeaeaeaeaeaeaeaeae aeaeaeaeaeaeaeaeaeaeaeaeaeaeaeaeaeaeaeaeaeaeaeaeaeaeaeaeaeaeaeaestivalis*) * We listen to you, Elder Flax-leaf Ankle-aster (*Ionactis linariifolia*) * We revere you, Elder Hop Sedge (*Carex lupulina*) * We praise you, Elder Forked pppppppppppppppppppppppppppppppppppppppppppp ppppppppppppppppppppppppppppppppppppppppppPanic Grass (*Dichanthelium dichotomum*) * We belong to you, Elder cccccccccccccccccccccccccccccccccccccccccccccccccccccccccccccccccccc ccccccccccCoralbean (*Erythrina herbacea*) * We thank you, Elder Roundpod St. John's Wort (*Hypericum cistifolium*) * We kneel before you, Elder Celery-leaf bbbbbbbbbbbbbbbbbbbbbbbb bbbbbbbbbbbbbbbbbbbbbbbbbbbbbbbbbbbbbbbbbbbbbbbbbbbbbbbbbbbbbbbbbbbbbbbbbbbbbbbb bbbbbbbbbbbbbbbbbbbbbbbbbbbbbbbbbbbbbbbbbbbbbbbbbbbbbbbbbbbbbbbbbbbbbbbbbbbbbbbb bbbbbbbbbbbbbbbbbbbbbbbbbbbbbbbbbbbbbbbbbbbbbbbbbbbbbbbbbbbbbbbbbbbbbbbbbbbbbbbb bbbbbbbbbbbbbbbbbbbbButtercup (*Ranunculus sceleratus*) * We revere you, Elder Flax-leaf

Fleabane (*Conyza bbbbbbbbbbbbbbbbbbbbbbbbbbbbbbbbbbbbbbbbbbbbbbbbbbbbbbbbbonariensis*) * We listen to you, Elder Water Oak (*ququququququququququququququququququququququququq uqququququQuercus nigra*) * We need you, Elder Sacred Lotus (*Nelumbo nucifera*) * We bow before you, Elder Spotted St. John's Wort (*Hypericum ppppppppppppppppppppppppppppppppppppppppp pppppppppppppppppppppppppppppppppppppunctatum*) * We belong to you, Elder tttttttttttttttttttttttttttt tttttttttttttttttttttttttttttttttttttttttttttttttttttttttTtoothache Grass (*Ctenium aromaticum*) * We worship you, Elder Southern Blue Flag (*Iris virginica*) * We revere you, Elder White Spikerush (*Eleocharis albida*) * We praise you, Elder Fascicled Beaksedge (*Rhynchospora fascicularis*) * We listen to you, Elder ccccccccccccccccccccccccccccccccccccccccccccccccccccccccccccccccccccccccc cccccccCoastal bbbbbbbbbbbbbbbbbbbbbbbbbbbbbbbbbbbbbbbbbbbbbbbbbbbbbbbbbbbbbbbbbbbbb bbbbbbbbbbbbbbbbbbbbbbbbbbbbbbbbbbbbbbbbbbbbbb Bedstraw (*Galium hhhhhhhhhhhhhhhh hhhhhhhhhhhhhhhhhhhhhhhhhhhhhhhhhhhhhhhhhhhhhispidulum*) * We listen to you, Elder bbbbb bbbbbbbbbbbbbbbbbbbbbbbbbbbbbbbbbbbbbbbbbbbbbbbbbbbbbbbbbbbbbbbbbbbbbbbbbbbbbbbbbbbb bbbbbbbbbbbbbbbbbbbbbbbbbbbbbbbbbbbbbbbbbbbbbbbbbbbbbbbbbbbbbbbbbbbbbbbbbbbbbbbbbbbbbbbbb bbbbbbbbbbbbbbbbbbbbBuckthorn bbbbbbbbbbbbbbbbbbbbbbbbbbbbbbbbbbbbbbbbbbbbbbbbbbbbbb bbbbbbbbbbbbbbbbbbbbbbbbbbbbbbbbbbbbbbbbbbbbbbbbbbbbbbbbbbbbbbbbbbbbbbbbbbbbbbbbbbbbbb bbbbbbbbbbbbbbbbbbbBully (*Sideroxylon lycioides*) * We need you, eeeeeeeeeeeeeeeeeeeeeeeeee eeeeeeeeElder Black Needlerush (*jjjjjjjjjjjjjjjjjjjjjjjjjjjjjjjjjjjjjjjjjjjjjjjjjjjjjjjjjjjjjjjjjjjjJuncus roemerianus*) * We adore you, Elder Saltmarsh Cordgrass (*Spartina alterniflora*) * We listen to you, Elder ttttttttttttttttttttt ttttttttttttttttttttttttttttttttttttttttttttttttttttttttttttttttttttttttTurkey Oak (*ququququququququququququququq uQuercus laevis*) * We venerate you, Elder ppppppppppppppppppppppppppppppppppppppppppppppppp pppppppppppppppppppppppppppppppppppppppppppppppppppppppppppppppppppppppppppppppppppppppppppppP eppermint (*Mentha x pppppppppppppppppppppppppppppppppppppppppppppppppppppppppppppppppppppppppp pppppppppppppppppiperita*) * We thank you, Elder Arrowleaf ttttttttttttttttttttttttttttttttttttttttTearthu mb (*pppppppppppppppppppppppppppppppppppppppppPolygonum sagittatum*) * We love you, Elder Fringed Yelloweyed Grass (*Xyris fffffffffffffffffffffffffffffffffffffffffffffffffffffffffffffffffffffffffffffffffffffffffffffffffffffffffffffffffffffffimbriata*) * We need you, Elder Velvetleaf Ticktrtrtrtrtrtrtrtrtrtrtrtrtrtrtrefoil (*Desmodium vvvvv vvvvvvvvvvvvvvvvvvvvvvvvvvvvviridiflorum*) * We bow before you, Elder Eastern Silver Aster (*Symphyotrichum ccccccccccccccccccccccccccccccccccccccccccccccccccccccccccccccccccconcolor*) * We belong to you, Elder Hair Grass (*Eleocharis bbbbbbbbbbbbbbbbbbbbbbbbbbbbbbbbbbbbbbbbb bbbbbbbbbbbbbbbbbbbbbbbbbbbbbbbbbbbbbbbbbbbbbbbbbbbbbbbbbbbbbbbbbbbbbbbaldwinii*) * We worship you, Elder Southern Sandbur (*Cenchrus echinatus*) * We kneel before you, Elder bbbbbbbbbbbbbbb bbbbbbbbbbbbbbbbbbbbbbbbbbbbbbbbbbbbbbbbbbbbbbbbbbbbbbbbbbbbbbbbbbbbbbbbbbbbbbbbbbbbbbbbbb bbbbbbbbbbbbbbbbbbbbbbbbbbbbbbbbbbbbbbbbbBuffalo Bur (*Solanum rostratum*) * We listen to you, Elder Fragrant Snakeroot (*Ageratina hhhhhhhhhhhherbacea*) *   We love you, Elder Thymeleaf Sandwort (*Arenaria sssssssssssssssssssssssssssssssssssssssssssssssssssssssssssssssssssssssssssss ssssssssssssssssssssssssssssssssserpyllifolia*) * We praise you, Elder Swamp Sunflower (*Helianthus angustifolius*) * We belong to you, Elder Round-fruited ppppppppppppppppppppppppppppppp ppppppppppppppppppppppppppppppppppppppppppppppppppppppppppppppppppppppppppppppppp ppppppppppppppppppppppppppppppppppppppppppppppppppppppppppppppppppppppppppppppppp ppppppppppppppppppppppppppppppppppppppPanic Grass (*Dichanthelium sphaerocarpon*) * We kneel before you, Elder Nakedflower Ticktrtrtrtrtrtrtrtrtrtrtrefoil (*Desmodium nudiflorum*) * We revere you, Elder trtrtrtrtrtrtrtrtrtrtrtrtrtrtrtrtrtrtrtrtrtrtrtrtrtrtrtrtrtrtrtrtrt rtrtrtrtrtrtrtrtrtrtrtrtrtrtrtrtrtrTread Softly (*Cnidoscolus stimulosus*) * We worship you, Elder bbbbbbbbbbbbbbbbbbbbbbbbbbbbbbbbbbbbbbbbbbbbbbbbbbbbbbbbbbbbbbBermuda   Grass (*Cynodon dactylon*) * We belong to you, Elder Straw-colored Flat Sedge (*Cyperus strstrstrstrstr strstrstrstrstrstrstrstrigosus*) * We praise you, Elder Bigleaf Magnolia (*Magnolia macrophylla*) * We kneel before you, Elder Salt Bush (*bbbbbbbbbbbbbbbbbbbbbbbbbbbbbbbbbbbbbbbbbbbbbbbbbbbbbbbbbbb bbbbbbbbbbbbbbbbbbbbbbbbbbbbbbbbbbbbbbbBaccharis halimifolia*) * We love you, Elder Ramie (*Boehmeria nivea*) * We worship you, Elder Swamp Flat Sedge (*Cyperus dddddddddddddddddddd dddddddddddddddddddddddddddddddddddddddddddddddddddddddddddddddddddddddddddddddddd dddddddddddddddddddddddddistinctus*) * We belong to you, Elder Shortleaf Sundew (*Drosera brbrbrbrbrbrbrbrbrbrbrbrevifolia)* We praise you, Elder Common Leopardbane (*Arnica acaulis*) * We thank you, Elder White Doll's Daisy (*Boltonia asteroides*) * We bow before you, Elder Black Walnut (*Juglans nigra*) *   We love you, Elder ccccccccccccccccccccccccccccccccccccccccccccccccc Coffeeweed (*Sesbania herbacea*) * We need you, Elder Lamb's Quarters (*chchchchchchchchc hchchchchchchchchchchchchchchchchchchchchchChenopodium album*) * We listen to you, Elder Seabeach ooooooooooooOrach (*Atriplex mucronata*) * We bow before you, Elder Carolina Ponyfoot (*Dichondra carolinensis)* We belong to you, Elder Green Adder's-mouth Orchid (*Malaxis unifolia*) * We worship you, Elder grgrgrgrgrgrgrgrgrgrgrgrgrgrgrgrgrgrgrgrgrgrgrgrgrgr grgrgrgrgrgrgrgrgrgrgrgrgrgrgrgrgrgrgrgrgrgrgrgrgrgrgrgrgrgrgrgrgrgrgrgrgrgrgrgrgr Grassleaf Lettuce (*Lactuca grgrgrgrgrgrgrgrgrgrgraminifolia*) * We revere you, Elder Virginia plpl plplplplplplplplplplplplplplplplplplplplplplplplplplplplplplplplplplplplplplPlanta-in (*Plantago virginica*) * We praise you, Elder Sand Ticktrtrtrtrtrtrtrtrtrtrtrtrtrtrtrtrtrtrtrt rtrtrtrtrtrtrtrtrtrefoil (*Desmodium lineatum*) * We belong to you, Elder Toothed White-Topped Aster (*Sericocarpus asteroides*) * We revere you, Elder Swamp Sweetbells (*Eubotrys racemosa*) * We love you, Elder White Sweet Clover (*Melilotus albus*) * We praise you, Elder Blue tttttttttttttttttttttttttttttttttttttttttttttttttttttttttttttttttttttttttttttttttttToadflax (*Nuttallanthus ccccccc

cccccccccccccccccccccccccccccccccccccccccccccccccccccccccccccccccccccccccccccccccccccccccccccccccccccccccccc
ccccccccccccccccccccccccccccccccccccccccccccccccccccccanadensis) * We worship you, Elder ddddddddddd
ddddddddddddddddddddddddddddddddddddddddddddddddddDallisgrass (*Paspalum dilatatum*) *
We revere you, Elder Floating Marshpppppppppppppppppppppppppppppppppppppppppppppppppppppppp
ppppppppppppppppppppppppppppppppppppppppppppennywor (*Hydrocotyle ranunculoides*) * We
praise you, Elder Southern Wedgegrass (*sphsphsphsphsphsphsphsphsphsphsphsphsphsphsphsph*
Sphenopholis ffffffffffffffffffffffffffffffiliformis) * We love you, Elder Blue Waterhyssop (*Bacopa*
cccccccccccccccccccccccccccccccccccccccccccccccccccccccccccccccccccccccccccccccccccccccccccccaroliniana) * We
need you, Elder Indigo Bush (*Amorpha fruticosa*) * We worship you, Elder Sea Daisy (*Borrichia*
frutescens) * We listen to you, Elder Trailing Fuzzybean (*Strophostyles helvola*) * We kneel before
you, Elder Narrowleaf ppppppppppppppppppppppppppppppppppppppppPurple Everlasting
(*Gamochaeta falcata*) * We belong to you, Elder Bog Smartweed (*Persicaria setacea*) * We bow
before you, Elder Hairy Smartweed (*Persicaria hirsuta*) * We praise you, Elder Dune Sandbur
(*Cenchrus trtrtrtrtrtrtrtrtrtrtrtrtrtribuloides*) * We worship you, Elder Canada gggggggggggggg
gggggggggggggggggggggggggGermander (*ttttttttttttttttttttttttttttttttttttttttTeucrium ccccccccccccccccccccccccccan*
adense) * We need you, Elder Gaping Grass (*Steinchisma hians*) * We listen to you, Elder
Savannah Hairgrass (*Muhlenbergia expansa*) * We love you, Elder Desert Horse-ppppp
pppppppppppppppppppppppppppppppppppppppppppppppppppppppppppppppppppppppppppppppppppppppppppppp
ppurslane (*Trianthema ppppppppppppppppppppppppppppppppppppppppppppppppppppppportulacastrum*) * We
revere you, Elder Rosepink (*Sabatia angularis*) * We worship you, Elder Crimson Clover
(*Trifolium incarnatum*) * We belong to you, Elder Fireweed (*Erechtites hhhhhhhhhhhhhhhhh*
hhhhhhhhhhhhhhhhhhieraciifolius) * We praise you, Elder ddddddddddddddddddddddddddddd
ddddddddddddddddddddddddddddddddddddddddddddddddddddddddddddddddddddddddddddddddddddddddddd
dddddddddddddddddddddddddddddddddddddddddddddddddddddddddddddddddddddddDeciduous Holly (*Ilex*
dddddddddddddddddddddddddddddddddddddddecidua) * We bow before you, Elder Saltmarsh
Fingergrass (*Eustachys glauca*) * We venerate you, Elder Sparrow Vetch (*Vicia (ttttttttttttttttttttttt*
tttttttttttttttttttttttttttttttttttttttttttttttttetrasperma) * We listen to you, Elder Tall Yelloweyed Grass
(*Xyris plplplplplplplplplplplplplplplplplplplplplplplplplplplplplplplplplplplplplplplplplplplplplpl*
platylepis) * We love you, Elder Black Cherry (*Prunus serotina*) * We bow before you, Elder
Sand-swamp Whitetop (*Rhynchospora latifolia*) * We praise you, Elder Redbud (*Cercis ccccccccc*
cccccccccccccccccccccccccccccccccccccccccccccccccccanadensis) * We listen to you, Elder ccccccccccccc
cccccccccccccccccccccccccccccccccCamphorweed (*Heterotheca subaxillaris*) * We learn from you,
Elder Winged Sumac (*Rhus ccccccccccccccccccccccccccccccccccccccccccccccccccccccccccccccccopallinum*) *
We praise you, Elder Western Tansymustard (*Descurainia ppppppppppppppppppppppppppppppppppp*

ppppppppppppppppppppppppppppppppppppppppppppppppppppppppppppppppppppppppppppinnata) * We kneel before you, Elder Lanceleaf Rose Gentian (*Sabatia difformis*) * We worship you, Elder Swamp ttttttttttttttttttttttttttttttttttttttttttttttttttttttttttttttttttttttttttttttttTupelo (*Nyssa biflora*) * We revere you, Elder Tidal-marsh Water-hemp (*Amaranthus cccccccccccccccccccccccccccccccccccccc ccccccccannabinus*) * We bow before you, Elder Florida Shieldfern (*Dryopteris ludoviciana*) * We belong to you, Elder Climbing Buckthorn (*Sageretia minutiflora*) * We thank you, Elder Oppositeleaf Sunflower (*Acmella repens*) * We love you, Elder Marsh Rose Gentian (*Sabatia ddddddddddddddddddddddddddddddddddddddddddddddddddddddddddddddddddddddddddddddddddd ddddddddddddddddddddddddddddddddddddddddddddddddddddddddodecandra*) * We need you, Elder Cutleaf Watermilfoil (*Myriophyllum ppppppppppppppppppppppppppppppppppppppppppppppppppppppppppp ppppppppppppppppppppppppppppppppppppppppppppppppppppppppppppppppppppppppppppppppppinnatum*) * We worship you, Elder Field Dodder (*Cuscuta ccccccccccccccccccccccccccccccccccccccccccccccccccccccccc cccccampestris*) * We kneel before you, Elder Spearmint (*Mentha spicata*) * We praise you, Elder Hirsute Sedge (*Carex cccccccccccccccccccccccccccccccccccccccccccccccccccccomplanata*) * We listen to you, Elder Heartwing Sorrel (*Rumex hhhhhhhhhhhhhhhhhhhhhhhhhhhhhhhhhhhhhhhhhhhhhastatulus*) * We need you, Elder Staggerbush (*Lyonia mariana*) * We worship you, Elder Fragrant Water-lily (*Nymphaea odorata*) * We revere you, Elder Crowned bbbbbbbbbbbbbbbbbbbbbbbbbbbbbbbbbbbb bbbbbbbbbbbbbbbbbbbbbbbbbbbbbbbbbbbbbbbbbbbbbbbbbbbbbbbbbbbbbbbbbbbbbbbbbbbbbbbbbbbbbb bbbbbbbbbbbbbbbbbbbbbbbbbbbbbbbbbbbbbbbbbbbbbbbbbbbbbbbbbbbbbbbbbbbbbbbbbbbbbbbbbbbbbb bbbBeggarticks (*Bidens trichosperma*) * We honor you, Elder Rabbit ttttttttttttttttttttttttttttttttttt tttttttttttttttttttttttttttttttttttttttttttttttTobacco (*Pseudognaphalium obtusifolium*) * We belong to you, Elder Foxtail Bog Club-moss (*Lycopodiella alopecuroides*) * We love you, Elder Common Goldstar (*Hypoxis micrantha*) * We praise you, Elder Hog Apple crcrcrcrcrcrcrcrcrcrcrcrcrcrcrcr crcrcrcrcrcrcrcrcrcrcrcrcrcrcrcrcrcrcrcrcrcrcrcrcrcrcrCrataegus   (*crcrcrcrcrcrcrcrcrcrcrcrcrcr crus-galli*) * We bow before you, Elder Quail Plant (*Heliotropium ccccccccccccccccccccccccccccccccc cccccccccccccccccccccccccccccccccccccccccccccccccccccccccccccccccccccccurassavicum*) * We belong to you, Elder Spurred bbbbbbbbbbbbbbbbbbbbbbbbbbbbbbbbbbbbbbbbbbbbbbbbbbbbbbbbbbbbbbbbbbbbbb bbbbbbbbbbbbbbbbbbbbbbbbButterfly Pea (*Centrosema vvvvvvvvvvvvvvvvvvvvvvvvvirginianum*) * We honor you, Elder Mountain aaaaaaaaaaaaaaaaaaaaaaaaaaaaaaaaaaaaaaaaaaaaaaaaaaaaaaaaaaaaaaaaaaaa aaaaaaaaaaaaaaaaaaAzalea (*Rhododendron ccccccccccccccccccccccccccccccccccccccccccccccccccccccccccc ccccccccccccccccccccccccccccccccccccanescens*) * We need you, Elder Florida Sand Plum (*Prunus angustifolia*) * We bow before you, Elder Cinnamon Fern (*Osmunda cinnamomea*) * We praise you, Elder Giant Duckweed (*Spirodela pppppppppppppppppppppppppppppppppppppppppppppppppppppppppppppppp ppppppppppppppppppppppppppppppppppppppppppppppppppppppppppppppppppppppppppppolyrrhiza*) * We worship you, Elder Bearded grgrgrgrgrgrgrgrgrgrgrgrgrgrgrgrgrgrgrgrgrgrgrgrgrgrgrgrgrgrgrgrgrgrgr grgrgrgrgrgrgrgrgrgrgrgrgrgrgrgrgrgrgrGrasspink (*Calopogon barbatus*) * We kneel before you, Elder Downy Milkpea (*Galactia volubilis*) * We need you, Elder Creeping Blueberry (*Vaccinium   crcrcrcrcrcrcrcrcrcrcrcrcrcrcrcrcrcrcrcrcrcrcrcrcrcrcrcrcrcrcrcrcrcrcrcrcrcrassifolium*) * We honor you, Elder Slender Sea pppppppppppppppppppppppppppppppppppppppppppppppppppppppppp pppppppppppppppppppppppppppppppppppppppppppppppppppppppppppppppppppppppppppppppppppppppp pppppppppppppppPurslane (*Sesuvium maritimum*) * We belong to you, Elder Yellow Wild Indigo (*Baptisia* tttttttttttttttttttttttttttttttttttttttttttttttttttttttttttttttttttttttttttttttttttttt*inctoria*) * We revere you, Elder Pink-scale Gayfeather (*Liatris eeeeeeeeeeeelegans*) * We bow before you, Elder Spring Vetch (*Vicia lathyroides*) * We listen to you, Elder Devil's bbbbbbbbbbbbbbbbbbbbbbbbbbbbbb

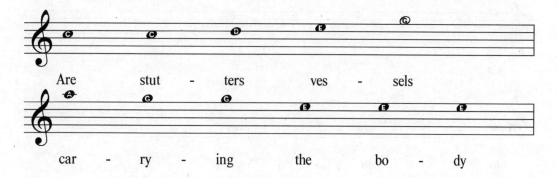

Are   stut   -   ters   ves   -   sels

car   -   ry   -   ing   the   bo   -   dy

bbbbbbbbbbbbbbbbbbbbbbbbbbbbbbbbbbbbbbbbbbbbbbbbbbbbbbbbbbbbbbbbbbbbbbbbbbbbbbbbbbbbbbbbbbbbbbbbbb Beggarticks (*Bidens frondosa*) * We honor you, Elder Twisted Tick Trefoil (*Desmodium tttttttttttttttttttttttttttttttttttttttttttttttttttttttttttttttttttttttttttttttttttt*tortuosum*) * We thank you, Elder Chaffweed (*Anagallis minima*) * We love you, Elder Knotroot Bristlegrass (*Setaria ppppppppppppppppppppppppppppppppppppppppppppppppppppppppppppppppppppppppppppppppppppppppppppp ppppppppppppppppppppppppppppppppppppppppppp*parviflora*) * We need you, Elder Lowland Rotala (*Rotala* rrrrrrrrrrrrrrrrrrrrrrrrrrrrrrrrrrrrrrrrrrrrrrrrrrrr*ramosior*) * We kneel before you, Elder Bay Star-Vine (*Schisandra glabra*) * We revere you, Elder Poison Ivy (*Toxicodendron radicans*) * We worship you, Elder Sour Clover (*Melilotus indicus*) * We love you, Elder Glowing Nightshade (*Solanum pseudog*rgrgrgrgrgrgrgrgrgrgrgrgrgrgrgrgrgrgrgrgrgrgrgrgrgrgrgrgr*acile*) * We listen to you, Elder Necklace pppppppppppppppppppppppppppppppppppppppppppppppppppppppppppppppppppppp ppppppppppppppppppppppppppppppppppppppppp*Poplar* (*Populus deltoides*) * We learn from you, Elder Carolina Yelloweyed Grass (*Xyris caroliniana*) * We bow before you, Elder Autumn blblb lblblblblblblblblblblblblblblblblblblblblblblblblblblblblblblblblblblblblblblblblblblblblblbl blBluegrass (*Poa autumnalis*) * We thank you, Elder Wiregrass (*Aristida stricta*) * We honor you, Elder Horseweed (*Conyza cccccccccccccccccccccccccccccccccccccccccccccccccccanadensis*) * We love you, Elder ccccccccccccccccccccccCanada Lettuce (*Lactuca ccccccccccccccccccccccccccccccccccccccccccccccccccccccccccanadensis*) * We need you, Elder Spanish Needles (*Bidens bipinnata*) * We belong to you, Elder Lady Lupine (*Lupinus villosus*) * We praise you, Elder Fringed Meadow Beauty (*Rhexia ppppppppppppppppppppppppppppppppppppppppppppppppppppppetiolata*) * We revere you, Elder American ccccccccccccccccccccccccccccccccccccccccccccccccccccccccccccccccccccccccccCupsca le (*Sacciolepis striata*) * We bow before you, Elder Smallfruit Spikerush (*Eleocharis microcarpa*) * We need you, Elder Cucumberleaf Sunflower (*Helianthus dddddddddddddddddddddddddddddd dddddddddddddddddddddddddddddddddddddddddddddddddddddddddddddddddddddddddddddddddddddd

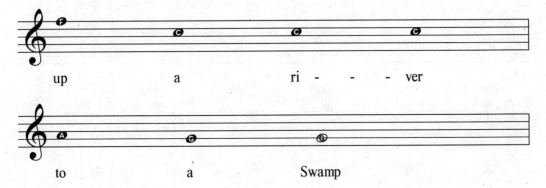

up   a   ri - - ver

to   a   Swamp

dddddddddddddddddddddddddddddddddddddddddddddddddddddddddddddddddddddebilis subsp. *cucumerifolius*) * We learn from you, Elder Hogwort (*Croton cccccccccccccccccccccccccccccccccccccccccccccccccccccapitatus*) * We listen to you, Elder Southern Green and Gold (*Chrysogonum virginianum var. australe*) * We worship you, Elder Fox Grape (*Vitis labrusca*) * We revere you, Elder Tough bbbbbbbbbbb bbbbbbbbbbbbbbbbbbbbbbbbbbbbbbbbbbbbbbbbbbbbbbbbbbbbbbbbbbbbbbbbbbbbbbbbbbbbbbbbbbbbbb bbbbbbbbbbbbbbbbbbbbbbbbbbbbbbbbbbbbbbbbbbbbbBully (*Sideroxylon ttttttttttttttttttttttttttttttttttt ttttttttttttttenax*) * We love you, Elder ccccccccccccccccccccccccccccccccccccccccccccccccccccccccccccc cccccccccccccccccccccccccccccccCoastal Doghobble (*Leucothoe axillaris*) * We listen to you, Elder Florida blblblblblblblblblblblblblblblblblblblblblblblblblblblblblblBluehearts (*Buchnera floridana*) * We bow before you, Elder Shortleaf (skskskskskskskskskskskskskskskSkeletongrass (*Gymnopogon brevifolius*) * We honor you, Elder Roundleaf Thoroughwort (*Eupatorium rotundifolium var. ovatum*) * We praise you, Elder Carolina Iris (*Iris hexagona*) * We belong to you, Elder Doorweed (*pppppppppppppppppppppppppppppppppppppppppppppppppppppppppppppppppppppppppppp ppppppppppppppppppppppppppppppppppppppppppppppppppppppppppppppppppppppppppppppppPolygonum *aviculare*) * We worship you, Elder Bracted Plantain (*Plantago aristata*) * We revere you, Elder clclclclclclclclclclclclclclclclclclclclclclclclclclclclclClustered Dock (*Rumex conglomeratus*) * We love you, Elder Arrowleaf Sida (*Sida rhombifolia*) * We listen to you, Elder Wrinkleleaf Goldenrod (*Solidago rugosa*) * We learn from you, Elder Sandpaper Vervain (*Verbena scabra*) * We thank you, Elder Yellow Crownbeard (*Verbesina oooooooooooooooooooooooooooooooooooo occidentalis*) * We praise you, Elder Whiteedge Flat Sedge (*Cyperus flflflflflflflflflflflflfl flavicomus*) * We love you, Elder ddddddddddddddddddddddddddddddddddddddddddddddd dddddddddddddddddddddddddddddddddddddddddddddddddddddddddddddddddddddddddddddddd dddddddddddddddddddddddddddddddddddddddDevil's Walking Stick (*Aralia spinosa*) * We revere you, Elder ccccccccccccccccccccccccccccccccccccccccccccccCinnamon Oak (*Quercus in-*

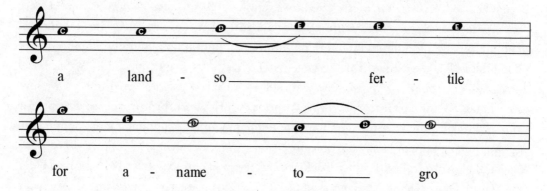

a land - so _____ fer - tile

for a - name - to _____ gro

cana) * We learn from you, Elder Narrowleaf prprprprprprprprprprprprprprprprprprprpr prprprprprprprprprprprprprprprprprprprprprprprPrimrose Willow (*Ludwigia linearis*) * We need you, Elder Slender bbbbbbbbbbbbbbbbbbbbbbbbbbbbbbbbbbbbbbbbbbbbbbbbbbbbbb bbbbbbbbbbbbbbbbbbbbbbbbbbbbbbbbbbbbbbbbbbbbBush-clover (*Lespedeza virginica*) * We worship you, Elder Dune grgrgrgrgrgrgrgrgrgrgrgrgrgrgrgrgrgrgrgrgrgrgrgrgrgrgrgrgrgrgrgr grgrgrgrgrgrgrgrgrgrgrgrgrgrgrgrgrgrgrgrgrgrgrgrgrgrgrgrgrgrgrgrGreenbriar (*Smilax auriculata*) * We honor you, Elder bbbbbbbbbbbbbbbbbbbbbbbbbbbbbbbbbbbbbbbbbbbbbbbbbbbbbbbbbbbb bbbbbbbbbbbbbbbbbbbbbbbbbbbbbbbbbbbbbbbbbbbbbbbbbbbbbbbbbbbbbbbbbbbbbbbbbbbbBitter weed (*Helenium amarum*) * We praise you, Elder Seacoast Bulrush (*Bolboschoenus robustus*) * We praise you, Elder Eagle Fern (*Pteridium aquilinum*) * We adore you, Elder Zigzag Bladderwort (*Utricularia subulata*) * We need you, Elder Slender Woodoats (*Chasmanthium laxum*) * We adore you, Elder Blood Sage (*Salvia cccccccccccccccccccccccccccccccccccccccccccccc cccccccccccccccccccccccccccccccccccccccccccccccccccccccccoccinea*) * We need you, Elder cccccccccccccccccccccccccccccccccccccccccccccccccccccccccccccccccccccccccccccCoastal

Serviceberry (*Amelanchier obovalis*) * We love you, Elder Southern bbbbbbbbbbbbbbbbbbbbbb bbbbbbbbbbbbbbbbbbbbbbbbbbbbbbbbbbbbbbbBeeblossom (*Oenothera simulans*) * We praise you, Elder Greater Tickseed (*Coreopsis major*) * We revere you, Elder Smutgrass (*Sporobolus indicus*) * We belong to you, Elder Sweet ppppppppppppppppppppppppppppppppppppppppppppppp pppppppppppppppppppppppppppppppppppppppppppppppppppppppppppppppppppppppppppppppppppp Pitcherplant (*Sarracenia rubra*) * We honor you, Elder Dwarf Greenbriar (*Smilax pppppppppppppppppppppppppppppppppppppppppppppppppppppppppppppppppppppppppppppppppppumi la*) * We kneel before you, Elder Maryland Golden-aster (*Chrysopsis mariana*) * We follow you, Elder crcrcrcrcrcrcrcrcrcrcrcrcrcrcrcrcrcrcrcrcrcrcrcrcrcrcrcrcrcrcrcrcrcrcrcrcrcrcrcrcrc rcrcrcrcrcrcrcrcrcrcrcrCreeping Rush (*Juncus repens*) * We bow before you, Elder Pine Barren Flat Sedge (*Cyperus retrorsus*) * We love you, Elder Sleepy cccccccccccccccccccccccccccc ccccccccccccccccccccccccccccccCatchfly (*Silene antirrhina*) * We admire you, Elder Greater blbl blblblblblblblblblblblblblblblblblblblblblblblblblblblblblblblblblblblblblblblblblblblblbl blblblblblblblBladder Sedge (*Carex intumescens*) * We learn from you, Elder Witch Hazel (Hamamelis virginiana) * We worship you, Elder Crabapple (Malus angustifolia) * We love you, Elder White prprprprprprprprprprprprprprprprprprprprprprprprprprprprprprprprpr prprprprPrickly ppppppppppppppppppppppppppppppppppppppppppppppppppppppppppppppppppppp pppppppppppppppppppppppPoppy (*Argemone albifolia*) * We revere you, Elder Frost Grape (*Vitis vulpina*) * We learn from you, Elder Blackjack Oak (*Quercus marilandica*) * We need you, Elder One-flower Cancer-Root (*Orobanche uniflora*) * We listen to you, Elder Showy Milkwort (*Asemeia grgrgrgrgrgrgrgrgrgrgrgrgrgrgrgrgrgrgrgrgrgrgrgrgrgrgrgrgrgrgrgrgrgrgrgrgrgrandiflora*) * We revere you, Elder Chinese (ppppppppppppppppppppppppppppppppppppppppppppppppppppppppppppp pppppppppppppppppppppppppppppppParasol Tree (*Firmiana simplex*) * We belong to you, Elder American Frogbit (*Limnobium spongia*) * We bow before you, Elder Coast Snowbell (*Styrax grandifolius*) * We praise you, Elder Sleeping Beauty (*Oxalis corniculata*) * We listen to you, Elder Soft Rush (*Juncus effusus*) * We kneel before you, Elder Low Pinebarren Milkwort (*ppppppppppppppppppppppppppppppppppppppppppppppppppppppppppppppppppppppppppppppppppppPolygala ramosa*) * We belong to you, Elder Smallflower Fumewort (*Corydalis micrantha* subsp. *australis*) * We worship you, Elder Bush ppppppppppppppppppppppppppppppppppppppppppppppppppppppppppppppp ppppppppppppppppppppppppppppppppppppppppppppppppppppppppppppppppppppppppppppppppppppPalmetto (*Sabal minor*) * We love you, Elder Dogfennel (*Eupatorium cccccccccccccccccccccccccccccccccccccccc ccccccccccccccccccccccccccccccccccccccccccccccccccccccccccccccccccccapillifolium*) * We kneel before you, Elder Yellowseed False ppppppppppppppppppppppppppppppppppppppppppppppppppppPimpernel (*Lindernia dubia*) * We need you, Elder Mayweed (*Anthemis cccccccccccccccccccccccccccccccccccccccccccccccccccc *cccccccccccccccccccccotula*) * We belong to you, Elder ppppppppppppppppppppppppppppppppppp pppppppppppppppppppppppppppppppppppPotato Dwarf Dandelion (*Krigia dandelion*) * We honor you, Elder Eastern Gamagrass (*Tripsacum dactyloides*) * We love you, Elder Blue Beech (*Carpinus ccccccccccccccccccccccccccccccccccccccccccccccccccccccccccccccccccccccccccccccccccccc ccccccccccccaroliniana*) * We honor you, Elder Beach False Foxglove (*Agalinis fasciculata*) * We revere you, Elder Marsh Fimbry (*Fimbristylis spadicea*) * We bow before you, Elder ccccccccccc cccccccccccccccccccccccccccccccccccccccccccccccccccccccccccccccccccccccccccccccccccccccc cCalico Aster (*Symphyotrichum lateriflorum*) * We adore you, Elder Inflated Narrow-leaf Sedge (*Carex grgrgrgrgrgrgrgrgrgrgrgrgrgrgrgrgrgrgrgrgrisea*) * We thank you, Elder ppppppppppppppppppppppppppppp pppppppppppppppppppppppppppppppppppppppppppppppppppppppppppppppppppppppppppppppppppppppppppp ppppppppppppppppppPeppervine (*Nekemias arborea*) * We need you, Elder Eastern Grasswort (*Lilaeopsis chchchchchchchchchchchchchchchchchchchchinensis*) * We belong to you, Elder Water Ash (*Fraxinus caroliniana*) * We praise you, Elder Northern Frogfruit (*Phyla lanceolata*) * We revere you, Elder Pond Cypress (*Taxodium distichum var. imbricarium*) * We honor you, Elder Rattlesnake Master (*Eryngium yuccifolium*) * We listen to you, Elder Glade Lobelia (*Lobelia glandulosa*) * We love you, Elder Willowleaf Goldenrod (*Solidago stricta*) * We admire you, Elder ppppppppppppppppppppppppppppppppppppppppppppppppppppppppppppppppppppppppppppppppppppp ppppppppppppppppppppppppppppppppppppppppppppppppppppppppppppPickerelweed (*Pontederia cordata*) * We belong to you, Elder Quaker Ladies (*Houstonia caerulea*) * We honor you, Elder Bog White Violet (*Viola lanceolata*) * We praise you, Elder Florida Pusley (*Richardia scabra*) * We bow before you, Elder Coast Amaranth (*Amaranthus ppppppppppppppppppppppppppppppppppppppppppppppppp pppppppppppppppppppppppppppppppppppppppppumilus*) * We listen to you, Elder Highbush blblblbl blblblblblblblblblblblblblblblblblblblblblblblblblblblblblblblblblblblblblblblblblblblblblblbl blblblblblblblblblblblblblblblblblblblblblblblblblblblblblblblblblblblblblblblblblblblblblblbl blblblblblblblblblblblblblblblblblblblblblblblblblblblblblblblblblblblblBlueberry (*Vaccinium ccc cccccccccccccccccccccccccccccccccccccccccccccccccccccccccccccccccccccccccccccccccccccccccccccc cccccccccorymbosum*) * We honor you, Elder bbbbbbbbbbbbbbbbbbbbbbbbbbbbbbbbbbbbbbbbbbbbb bbbbbbbbbbbbbbbbbbbbbbbbbbbbbbbbbbbbbbbbbbbbbbbbbbbbbbbbbbbbbbbbbbbbbbbbbbbbbbbbbbbb bbbbbbbbbbbbbbbbbbbbbbbbbbbbbbbbbbbbbbbbbbbbbbbbbbbbbbbbbbbbbbbbbbbbbbbbbbbbbBanana Lily (*Nymphaea mexicana*) * We kneel before you, Elder Carolina bbbbbbbbbbbbbbbbbbbbbbbbbbbbb bbbbbbbbbbbbbbbbbbbbbbbbbbbbbbbbbbbbbbbbbbbbbbbbbbbbbbbbbbbbbbbbbbbbbbbbbbbbbbbbbbbb bbbbbbbbbbbbbbbbbbbbbbbbbbbbbbbbButtercup (*Ranunculus ccccccccccccccccccccccccccccccc cccccccccccccccccccccccccccccccccccccccccccccccccccccccarolinianus*) * We learn from you, Elder Cottony Golden-aster (*Chrysopsis gggggggggggggggggggggggggggggggggggggggggggggggggggggggggggggggggggggggggggg ggggggggggggggggggggggggggggggggggggggggggggggggggggggggggggggggggggggggggggggggggggggggggggggggggggossypina) * We thank you, eeeeeeeeeeeee eeeeeeeeeeeeeeeeeeeeeElder Soft Elm (*Ulmus americana*) * We love you, Elder Black Medic (*Medicago lupulina*) * We need you, Elder Lily of the Valley Vine (*Salpichroa oooooooooooooooooooooooooriganifolia*) * We admire you, Elder Dangleberry (*ggggggggggggggggggg ggggggggggggggggggggggggggggggggggggggggggggggggggggggggggggggggggggggggggggGaylussacia frondosa*) * We praise you, Elder Coastal Rose Gentian (*Sabatia cccccccccccccccccccccccccccccccccccccccccccccc ccccccccccccccccccccccccccccccccccccccalycina*) * We honor you, Elder ppppppppppppppppppppppppppp ppppppppppppppppppppppppppppppppppppppppPurpletop (*Tridens flavus*) * We revere you, Elder Black-eyed Susan (*Rudbeckia hirta*) * We follow you, Elder Pineland Rayless Goldenrod (*bbbbbbbbbbbbbbbbbbbbbbbbbbbbbbbbbbbbbbbbbbbbbbbbbbbbbbbbbbbbbbbbbbbbbbbbbbbBigelowia nudata*) *

each   ker - nel   of   cof   -   fee   has   a   name

We worship you, Elder cccccccccccccccccccccCandy Weed (*ppppppppppppppppppppppppppppppppp ppppppppppppppppppppppppppppPolygala lutea*) * We bow before you, Elder Carolina Silverbell (*Halesia carolina*) * We worship you, Elder Humped blblblblblblblblblblblblblblblblblblblblblb lblblblblblblblblblblBladderwort (*Utricularia gggggggggggggggggggggggggggggggggggggggggggggggggggibba*) * We belong to you, Elder Florida ppppppppppppppppppppppppppppppppppppppppppppppppppppppp ppppppppppppPellitory (*Parietaria floridana*) * We revere you, Elder Hairy bbbbbbbbbbbbbbbbbbbbbbbbbbbbbbbbbbbbbbbbbbbbbbbbbbbbbbbbbbbbbbbbbbbbbbbbbbbbbbbbbbb bbbbbbBedstraw (*Galium ppppppppppppilosum*) * We follow you, Elder Narrowleaf Cattail (*Typha aaaaaaaaaaaaaaaaaaaaaaaaaaaaaaaaaaaaaaaaaaaaaaaaaaangustifolia*) * We admire you, Elder Broad Beech Fern (*Phegopteris hexagonoptera*) * We need you, Elder ppppppppppppppppppp ppppppppppppppppppppppPerennial Ryegrass (*Lolium ppppppppppppppppppppppppperenne*) * We listen tttttttttttto you, Elder Swamp Smartweed (*ppppppppppppppppppppppppppppppppppppppppp ppppppppppppppppppppppppppppppppppppppppppppppppppPersicaria hydropppppppppppppppppppppppppp pppppppppppppppppppppppppppiperoides*) * We learn from you, eeeeeeeeeeeeeeeeeeeeeeeeeeeeeeeeee eeeeeeeeeeeeeElder Red Maple (*aaaaaaaaaaaaaaaaaaaaaaaaaaaaaaaaaaaaaaaAcer rubrum*) * We revere you, Elder Hat Pins (*eeeeeeeeeeeeeeeeeeeeeeeEriocaulon compressum*) * We belong to you, Elder Sand Hickory (*Carya pallida*) * We kneel before you, Elder Yellow Butterwort (*Pinguicula lutea*) * We adore you, Elder Umbrella Tree (*Magnolia tripetala*) * We thank you, Elder Wand Mullein (*Verbascum virgatum*) * We learn from you, Elder Winged Loosestrife (*Lythrum alatum* *var. lanceolatum)* * We listen to you, Elder Grassleaf Rush *(Juncus marginatus)* * We admire you, Elder Coastal Carolina Spiderlily *(Hymenocallis crassifolia)* * We adore you, Elder Purple Passionflower *(Passiflora incarnata)* * We praise you, Elder Saltmarsh Sabatia *(Sabatia stellaris)* * We bow before you, Elder Persimmon *(Diospyros virginiana)* * We admire you, Elder Southern Thorn (Crataegus viridis) * We praise you, Elder Toad Rush *(Juncus bufonius)* * wwwwwwww wwwwwwwwwwwwwwWe follow you, Elder Green aaaaaaaaaaaArrow aaaaaaaaaaaaaaaaaaaaaaaa aaaaaaaaaaaaaaaaaaaaaaaaaaaaaaaaaaaaaaaaaaaaaArum *(ppppppppppppppppppppppppppppppppppp ppppppppppppppppppppppppppppppppppppppppppppppppppppppppppppppppppppppppppppppppppp ppppppppppppppppppPeltandra virginica)* * We learn from you, Elder pppppppppppppppppppppppp pppppppppppppppppppppppppppppppppppppppppppppppppppppppppppppppppppppppppppppppppppp

each   green - mor - ning   has   a   name

pppppppppppppppppppppppppppppppppProcession flflflflflFlower *(ppppppppppppppppppppppppppppp ppppppppppppppppppppppppppppppPolygala incarnata)* * We praise you, Elder spspspspspspsps pspspSpeckled Gourd *(Melothria pppppppppppppppppppppppppppppppppppppppppppppppppppppppppp pppppppppppendula)* * We honor you, Elder Southern Arrowwood *(Viburnum dddddddddddddddddd dddddddddddddddddddddddddddddddddddddddddddddddddddddddddddddddddddddddddddddddddddd ddddddddddentatum)* *We adore you, Elder Green Fly Orchid *(Epidendrum magnoliae)* * We bow before you, Elder Bog Yelloweyed Grass *(Xyris dddddddddddddddddddddddddddddddddddddddddd dddddddddddddddddddddddddddddddddddddddddddddddddddddddddddddddddddddddddddddddddddd dddddddddddddddddddddddddddddddddddddddddddddddddddddddddddddddddddddddifformis)* * We kneel bbbbbbbbbbbbbbbbbbbbbbbbbbbbbbbbbbbbbbbbbbbbbbbbbbbbbbbbbbbbbbbbbbbbbbbb bbbbbbbbbbbbbbbefore you, Elder Climbing ddddddddddddddddddddddddddddddddddddddddd ddddddDayflower *(cccccccccccccccccccccccccccccccccccccccccCommelina ddddddddddddddddd dddddddddddddddddddddddddddddddddddddddddddddddddddddddddddddddddddddddddddddddddddd dddddddddddiffusa)* * We need you, Elder River bbbbbbbbbbbbbbbbbbbbbbbbbbbbbbbbbbbbbbbb bbbbbbbbbbbbbbbbbbbbbbbbbbbbbbbbbbbbbbbbbbbbbbbbbbbbbbbbbbbbbbbbbbbbbbbbbbbbbbbbbbbb bbbbbbbbbbbbbbbbbbbbbbbbbbbbbbbbbbbbbbbbbbbbbbbbbbbbbbbbbbbbbbbbbbbbbbbbbbbbbbbbBir ch *(bbbbbbbbbbbbbbbbbbbbbbbbbbbbbbbbbbbbbbbbbbbbbBetula nigra)* * We love you, Elder Coastal brbrbrbrbrbrbrbrbrbrbrbrbrbrbrbrbrBristlegrass *(Setaria ccccccccccccccccccccccorrugata)* * We follow you, Elder Herb-of-grace *(bbbbbbbbbbbbbbbbbbbbbbbbbbbbbbbbbbbbBacopa monnieri)* * We

admire you, Elder St. ppppppppppppppppppppppppppppppppppppppppppppppppppppppppppppppp
Peter's Wort (*Hypericum crux-andreae*) * We kneel before you, Elder Annual Blue-eyed Grass
(*Sisyrinchium rosulatum*) * We listen to you, Elder Horned bbbbbbbbbbbbbbbbbbbbbbbbbbbbbb
bbbbbbbbbbbbbbbbbbbbbbbbbbbbbbbbbbbbbbbbbbbbbbbbbbbbbbbbbbbbbbbbbbbbbbbBeakrush
(*Rhynchospora corniculata*) * We belong to you, Elder ppppppppppppppppppppppppppppppppp
ppppppppppppppppppppppppppppppppppppppppppppppppppppppppPine Lily (*Lilium ccccccccccccccc
ccccccccatesbaei*) * We learn from you, Elder White-flowered Milkweed (*Asclepias variegata*) *
We thank you, Elder Savannah prprprprprprprprprprprprPrimrose Willow (*Ludwigia virgata*)
* We love you, Elder Needlepod Rush (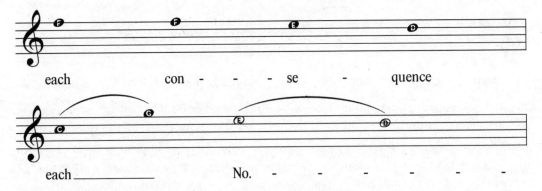*Juncus scirpoides*) * We
admire you, Elder dddddddddddddddddddddddddddddddddddDahoon (*Ilex ccccccccccccccccccccccc*

each   con - - - se - quence

each_____   No. - - - - - -

cassine) * We adore you, Elder Forked blblblblblblblblblblBluecurls (*trtrtrtrtrtrtrtrtrtrtrtrtrtrtr
trtrtrtrtrTrichostema dichotomum*) * We bow before you, Elder Hemp Dogbane (*Apocynum
cccccccccccccccccccccccccccccccccccccccccccccccccccccccccccccccccccccccccccccccannabinum*) * We
belong to you, Elder Curly Indigo (*Aeschynomene indica*) * We praise you, Elder Smooth
Elephantsfoot (*Elephantopus nudatus*) * We revere you, Elder Winter Bentgrass (*Agrostis
hyemalis*) * We honor you, Elder Violet Crabgrass (*Digitaria violascens*) * We need you, Elder
Carolina Wild ppppppppppppppppppppppppppppppppppppppppppppppppppppppppPetunia (*Ruellia
caroliniensis*) * We need you, Elder Appalachian ggggggggggggggggggggggggggggggggggggggggggg-
ggggggggggggggggggggggggggggggggggggggggggggggggggggGayfeather (*Liatris squarrulosa*) * We
need you, Elder Beach Evening prprprprprPrimrose (*Oenothera drdrdrdrdrdrdrdrdrdr
drummondii*) * We admire you, Elder Flax (*Linum uuuuuuuuuuuuuuuuuuuuuuuuuusitatissimum*) *
We adore you, Elder Small Black Blueberry (*Vaccinium tttttttttttttttttttttttttttttttttttttttenellum*) * We
follow you, Elder Pie Plant (*Eclipta prprprprprprprprprprprprprprprprprprprprprprprprprprprpr
prprostrata*) * We learn from you, Elder Toothed Rosinweed (*Silphium asteriscus var. dddddddd*

ddddddddddddddddddddddddddddddddddddddddddentatum) * We listen to you, Elder Littlehead Nutrush (*sclsclsclsclsclsclsclsclsclsclsclsclsclsclsclsclsclsclsclsclsclsclsclsclsclsclsclsclsclsclscl*) *Scleria oligantha*) * We thank you, Elder Southern Water Hemlock (*Cicuta mexicana*) * We admire you, Elder Groundnut (Apios americana) * We adore you, Elder Long-stalked grgrgr grgrgrgrgrgrgrgrgrgrgrgrgrgrgrgrgrgrgrgrgrgrgrgrgrgrgrgrgrgrgrgrgrgrgrgrgrgrgrGreenbriar (*Smilax pseudochina*) * We love you, Elder Shade Mudflower (*Micranthemum umbrosum*) * We follow you, Elder Slender Crabgrass (*Digitaria filiformis* var. *villosa*) * We belong to you, Elder Winter Grapefern (*bbbbbbbbbbbbbbbbbbbbbbbbbbbbbbbbbbbbbbbbbbbbbbbbbbbbbbbbBotrychium lunarioides*) * We praise you, Elder Needleleaf Rosette Grass (*Dichanthelium aciculare subsp. angustifolium*) * We admire you, Elder Climbing Dogbane (*trtrtrtrtrtrtrtrtrtrtrtrtrtr*

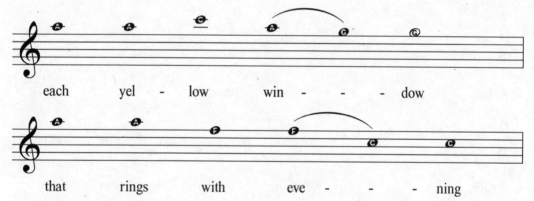

each   yel - low   win - - - dow

that   rings   with   eve - - - ning

Trachelospermum difforme) * We honor you, Elder Osceola's Plume (*Zigadenus ddddddddddddddd ddddddddddddddddddddddddddddddddddddddddddddddddddddddddddddddddddddddddddddddddddddd dddddddddddddddddddddddddddddddddddddddddddddddddensus*) * We bow before you, Elder Viperina (*Zornia brbrbrbrbrbrbrbrbrbrbrbrbrbrbrbrbracteata*) * We listen to you, Elder Millet Beaksedge (*Rhynchospora miliacea*) * We belong to you, Elder Southern Waxy Sedge (*Carex glaucescens*) * We admire you, bbbbbbbbbbbbbbbbbbbbbbbbbbbbbbbbbbbbbbbbbbbbbbbbbbbbbbbbbbbb bbbbbbbbbbbbbbbbbbbbbbbbbbbbbbbbbbbbbbbbbbbbbbbbbbbbbbbbbbbbbbbbbbbbbbbbbbbbbbbbbbbbbb bbbbbbbbbbbbbbbbbbbbbbbbbbbbbbbbbbbbbbbbbbbbbbbbbbbbbbbbbbbbbbbbbbbbbbbbbbbbbbbbbbbbbbbb bbbbbbbbbbbbbbbbbbbbbbbbbbbbbbbbbbbbbbbbbbbbbbbbbbbbbbbbbbbbbbbbbbbbbbbbbbbbbbbbbbbElder Butterweed (*Packera glglglglglglglglglglglglglglglglabella*) * We adore you, Elder False Willow (*Baccharis angustifolia*) * We listen to you, Elder Sand crcrcrcrcrcrcrcrcrcrcrcrcrcrcrcrcrcrcrc rcrcrcrcrcrCroton (*Croton glandulosus var. septentrionalis*) * We learn from you, Elder Early Yellowrocket (*Barbarea verna*) * We need you, Elder Drooping bbbbbbbbbbbbbbbbbbbbbbbbbbb bbbbbbbbbbbbbbbbbbbbbbbbbbbbbbbbbbbbbbbbbbbbbbbbbbbbbbbbbbbbbbbbbbbbbbbbbbbbbbbbbbbbbb bbbbbbbbbbbbbbbbbbBulrush (*Scirpus lineatus*) * We follow you, Elder Whiteheart Hickory (*ccccccccccCarya tttttttttttttomentosa*) * We love you, Elder Eastern Bluestar (*aaaaaaa aaaaaaaaaaaaaaaaaaaaaaaaaaaaaaaaaaaaaaaaaaaaaaaaaaaaaaaaaaaaaaaaaaaaaaAmsonia tabernaemontana* var. *salicifolia*) * We praise you, Elder Sword-leaf pppppppppppppppppppppp ppppppppppppppppppppppppppppppppppppppppppppppppppppppppppppppppppppppppppppppppppp ppppppppppppppPanic Grass (*Dichanthelium ensifolium*) * We belong to you, Elder cccccccccc cccccccccccccccccccccccccccccccccccccccccccccColicroot (*Aletris aurea*) * We revere you, Elder Wand ggggggggggggggggggggggggggggggggggggggggggggggggggggggGerardia (*Agalinis ppppppppppppppppppp pppppppppppppppppppppppppppppppppurpurea* var. *ppppppppppppppppppppppppppppppppppppppppppppppp purpurea*) * We listen to you, Elder Unicorn Root (*Aletris farinosa*) * We need you, Elder bbbbb

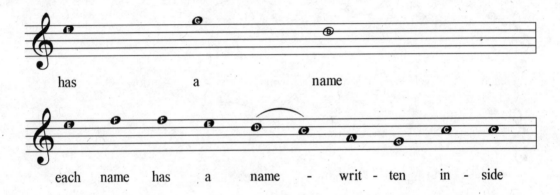

has   a   name

each name has a name - writ - ten in - side

bbbbbbbbbbbbbbbbbbbbbbbbbbbbbbbbbbbbbbbbbbbbbbbbbbbbbbbbbbbbbbbbbbbbbbbbbbbbbbbbbbb
bbbbbbbbbbbbbbbbbbbbbbbbbbbbbbbbbbbbbbbbbbbbbbbbbbbbbbbbbbbbbbbbbbbbbbbbbbbbbbbbbbb
bbbbbbbbbbbbbbbbbbbbbbbbbbbbbbbbbbbbbbbbbbbbbbbbbbbbbbbbbbbbbbbbbbbbbbbbbbbbbbbbbbb
bbbbbbbbbbbbbBasket Oak (*Quercus michauxii*) * We praise you, Elder Jumpseed (*Persicaria vv vvvvvvvvvvvvvvvvvvvvvvvvvvvvvvvvvvirginiana*) * We kneel before you, Elder Shadblow Serviceberry (*Amelanchier cccccccccccccccccccccccccccccccccanadensis*) * We learn from you, Elder Milk pppp ppppppppppppppppppppppppppppppppppppppppppppppPurslane (*Euphorbia maculata*) * We bow before you, Elder Moundlily Yucca (*Yucca gloriosa*) * We love you, Elder ccccccccccccCardinal Flower (*Lobelia cardinalis*) * We praise you, Elder Roughfruit Scaleseed (*Spermolepis dddddddd dddddddddddddddddddddddddddivaricata*) * We revere you, Elder Maryland Figwort (*Scrophularia marilandica*) * We belong to you, Elder White Edge Sedge (*Carex debilis*) * We follow you, Elder Bristly Greenbriar (*Smilax tamnoides*) * We learn from you, Elder Sandbog Death Camas (*Zigadenus glaberrimus*) * We thank you, Elder Southern Smilax (*Smilax smallii*) *

We listen to you, Elder Striped Wintergreen (ccccccccccccccccccccccccccccccccccccccccccccccccccccc ccccccccccccccccccccccccccccccccccccccChimaphila maculata) * We follow you, Elder Lopseed (Phryma leptostachya) * We bow before you, Elder Tapertip Rush (Juncus acuminatus) * We praise you, Elder Nutmeg Hickory (Carya myristiciformis) * We honor you, Elder Oldfield Cinquefoil (Potentilla simplex) * We admire you, Elder Whorled Marshpennywort (Hydrocotyle verticillata) * We belong to you, Elder St. Andrew's Cross (Hypericum hypericoides) * We need you, Elder Coral hhhhhhhhhhhhhhhhhhhhhhhhhhhhhhhhhhhhhhhhhhhhhhhhhhhhhhhhhhhhhhhhh hhhhhhhhhhhHoneysuckle (Lonicera sempervirens) * We revere you, Elder Pine Barren Goldenrod (Solidago fistulosa) * We belong to you, Elder Loblolly Pine (Pinus taeda) * We adore you, Elder Sand Post Oak (Quercus margarettae) * We kneel before you, Elder Cat Greenbriar (Smilax glauca) * We belong to you, Elder ppppppppppppppppppppppppppppppppppppppppPondspice (Litsea aestivalis) * We venerate you, Elder Marsh ppppppppppppppppppppppppppppppppppppp ppppppppppppppppppppppppppppppppppppppppPennywort (Hydrocotyle umbellata) * We learn from you, Elder Viviparous Spikerush (Eleocharis vivipara) * We worship you, Elder Windflower (Thalictrum thalictroides) * We adore you, Elder Smooth Solomon's Seal (ppppppppppppppppppppp ppppppppppppppppppppppppppppppppppppppppppppppppppppPolygonatum biflorum) * We venerate you, Elder Lizard's Tail (Saururus cernuus) * We belong to you, Elder Purple Bindweed (Ipomoea ccccccccccccccccccccccccccccccccccccccccccccccccccccccccccccordatotriloba var. cordatotriloba) * We kneel before you, Elder Backyard Strawberry (Duchesnea indica) * We worship you, Elder Hairy Beadgrass (Paspalum setaceum) * We belong to you, Elder Downy Lobelia (Lobelia ppppppppppppppppppppppppppppppppppppppppppppppppppppppppppppppppppppppppppppppppppppp pppppppuberula) * We adore you, Elder Annual Saltmarsh Aster (Symphyotrichum subulatum) * We belong to you, Elder Bog Hemp (Boehmeria cylindrica) * We venerate you, Elder Eastern Milkpea (Galactia regularis) * We worship you, Elder Poison Sumac (ttttttttttttttttttttttttttttttttttttt tttttttttToxicodendron vernix) * We praise you, Elder Vaseygrass (Paspalum urvillei) * We belong to you, Elder Swamp Dogwood (Cornus foemina) * We adore you, Elder Shaggy Hedgehyssop (Sophronanthe ppppppppppppppppppppppppppppppppppppppppppppppppppppppppppppppppppppppppppp ppppppppppppppppppppppppppppppppppilosa) * We love you, Elder Southern Dawnflower (Stylisma humistrata) * We kneel before you, Elder Carolina Bristlemallow (Modiola caroliniana) * We belong to you, Elder Smooth ppppppppppppppppppppppppppppppppppppppppppppppppppppppp pppppppppppPenstemon (Penstemon laevigatus) * We belong to you, Elder Forked Fimbry (Fimbristylis dichotoma) * We venerate you, Elder Peach (Prunus ppppppppppppppppppppppppppp ppppppppppersica) * We love you, Elder Seabeach Evening Primrose (Oenothera humifusa) * We worship you, Elder Camphor Pluchea (Pluchea camphorata) * We bow before you, Elder

Prostrate Blue Violet (*Viola walteri*) * We belong to you, Elder Swollen Bladderwort (*Utricularia inflata*) * We kneel before you, Elder Plumed Beaksedge (*Rhynchospora plumosa*) * We adore you, Elder Coral Greenbriar (*Smilax walteri*) * We belong to you, Elder Southern Lady Fern (*Athyrium filix-femina* var. *asplenioides*) * We praise you, Elder Florida Yam (*Dioscorea floridana*) * We learn from you, Elder Annual Bluegrass (*Poa annua*) * We belong to you, Elder Mistletoe (*Phoradendron leucarpum*) * We adore you, Elder Bunched Beaksedge (*Rhynchospora cephalantha*) * We love you, Elder Kidneyleaf Rosinweed (*Silphium compositum*) * We venerate you, Elder Hairy Chaffhead (*Carphephorus paniculatus*) * We belong to you, Elder American Hazelnut (*Corylus americana*) * We bow before you, Elder Maryland Milkwort (ppppppppppppppppppppppppppppppppppppp*Polygala mariana*) * We worship you, Elder Woodland Pinkroot (*Spigelia marilandica*) * We kneel before you, Elder Prairie Wedgegrass (*Sphenopholis obtusata*) * We belong to you, Elder White Poplar (*Populus alba*) * We belong to you, Elder Forked Rush (*Juncus dichotomus*) * We adore you, Elder Silky Sassafras (*Sassafras albidum*) * We praise you, Elder Carolina Geranium (*Geranium carolinianum*) * We love you, Elder Sugar Hackberry (*Celtis laevigata*) * We learn from you, Elder Softstem Bulrush (*Schoenoplectus tabernaemontani*) * We belong to you, Elder Slender Goldentop (*Euthamia caroliniana*) * We belong to you, Elder Pink Evening Primrose (*Oenothera speciosa*) * We worship you, Elder Wing-cup Water Primrose (*Ludwigia alata*) * We kneel before you, Elder Hairyfruit Chervil (*Chaerophyllum tainturieri*) * We bow before you, Elder Wood bbbbbbbbbbbbbbbbbbbbbbbbbbb bbbbbbbbbbbbbbbbbbbbbBetony (pppppppppppppppppppppppppppppppppppppppppppppppppppppppppppp ppp*Pedicularis canadensis*) * We adore you, Elder Stave Oak (*Quercus alba*) * We belong to you, Elder Asparagus (*Asparagus officinalis*) * We learn from you, Elder Wild Poinsettia (*Euphorbia heterophylla*) * We belong to you, Elder Coastal Salt Grass (*Distichlis spicata*) * We praise you, Elder jjjjjjjjjjjjjjjjjjjjjjjjjjjjjjjjjjjjjjjjjjjjjjjjjjjjjjjjjjjjjjjjjjjjjjjjjjjjjjjjjjjjJamaican Weed (Nama jjjjjjjjjjjjjjjjjjjjj *jamaicense*) * We adore you, Elder Rain Lily (*Zephyranthes atamasca*) * We love you, Elder Bull Crown Grass (ppppppppppppppppppppppppppppppppppppppppppppppppppppppppppppppp*Paspalum* (bbbbbb bbbbbbbbbbbbbbbbbbbbbbbbbbbbbbbbbbbbbbbbbbbbbbbbbbbb*boscianum*) * We belong to you, Elder Sticky Mouse-ear chchchchchchchchchchchchchchchchChickweed (*Cerastium glomeratum*) * We belong to you, Elder chchchchchchchchchchchchChinquapin (*Castanea* pppppppppppppppppp pppppppp*pumila*) * We kneel before you, Elder Wavyleaf Noseburn (*Tragia urens*) * We worship you, Elder Evergreen bbbbbbbbbbbbbbbbbbbbbbbbbbbbbbbbbbbbbbbbbbbbbbbbbbbbbbbbbbbbbbbbbbbbbbb bbbbbbbbbbbbbbbbbbbbbbbbbbbbbbbbbbbbbbbbbbbbbbbbbbbbbbbbbbbbbbbbbbbbbbbbbbbbbbbbbbbb bbbbbbbbbbbbbbbbbbbbbbbbbbbbbbbbbbbbbbbbbbbbbBayberry (*Myrica hhhhhhhhhhhhhhhh-hhhhhhhhhhhhhhhhhhheterophylla*) * We belong to you, Elder Tall Ironweed (Vernonia angustifolia) * We adore you, Elder Floating Mannagrass (*glglglglglglglglglglglGlyceria septentrionalis*) * We belong to you, Elder Seacoast Marsh Elder (*Iva iiiiiiiiiiiiiiiiiiiiiiiiiiiiiiiiiiiiiiiiiiiiiiiiiimbricata*) * We venerate you, Elder Carpet bbbbbbbbbbbbbbbbbbbbbbbbbbbbbbbbbbbbbbbbbbbbbbbbbbbbbb bbbbbbbbbbbbbbbbbbbbbbbbbbbbbbbbbbbbbbbbbbbbbbbbbbbbbbbbbbbbbbbbbbbbbbbbbbbbbbbbbbb bbbbbbbbbbbbbbbbbbbbbbbbbbbbbbbbbbbBurrweed (*Soliva stolonifera*) * We belong to you, Elder Twoleaf Watermilfoil (*Myriophyllum hhhhhhhhhhhhhhhhhhhhhhhhhhhhhhhhhhhhhh hhhhhhhhhhhhhhhhhhhhhhhhhhhhhheterophyllum*) * We adore you, Elder Arkansas Soft Pine (*pppppppppppppppppppppppppppppppppppppppppppppppppppppppppppppppppppppppPinus echinata*) * We love you, Elder Primrose-leaved Violet (*Viola prprprprprprprprprprprprprprprprprprprpr prprprprprprprprprprprprprimulifolia*) * We praise you, Elder ppppppppppppppppppppppppppppp ppppppppppppppppppppppppPopcorn Tree (*Triadica sebifera*) * We learn from you, Elder bbbbbbb bbbbbbbbbbbbbbbbbbbbbbbbbbbbbbbbbbbbbbbbbbbbbbbbbbbbbbbbbbbbbbbbbbbbbbbbbbbbbbbbbbbb bbbbbbbbbbbbbbbbbbbbbbbbbbbbbbbbbbbBeautyberry (*cccccccccccccccccccccccccccccccccccccccc ccccccccccccccccccccccccccCallicarpa americana*) * We kneel before you, Elder vvvvvvvvvvvvvvvvvvvvvvVenus Flytrap (*Dionaea muscipula*) * We bow before you, Elder Green cccccccccccccccccccccccCarpetweed (*Mollugo verticillata*) * We worship you, Elder Little (*blblb lblblblblblblblblblblblblblblblblblblblblblblblblblblblblblblblblblblblblblblblbl*) Bluestem (*Schizachyrium scoparium*) * We belong to you, Elder Clustered Beaksedge (*Rhynchospora glomerata*) * We adore you, Elder Sensitive Pea (*chchchchchchchchchchchchchchchchchchchch chchchchchchchchchchchchchchchchchchchchchchchchchchchchchchchChamaecrista nictitans*) * We belong to you, Elder Wild Yam (*dddddddddddddddddddddddddddddddddddddddddddddddddd dddddddddddddddddddddddddddddddddddddddddddddddddddddddddddddddddddddddddddddddddd ddddddddddddddddddddddDioscorea villosa*) * We love you, Elder Small Spikerush (*Eleocharis ppppppppppppppppppppppppppppppppppppparvula*) * We belong to you, Elder Giant brbrbrbrbrbrbr brbrbrbrbrbrbrbrBristlegrass (*Setaria magna*) * We venerate you, Elder Slimpod Rush (*Juncus dddddddddddddddddddddddddddddddddddddddddddddddddddddddddddddddddddddiffusissimus*) * We kneel before you, Elder Hedge Bindweed (*Calystegia sepium*) * We belong to you, Elder tttttttttt tttttttttttttttttttttttttttttttttttttttttttttttttttTeasel Sedge (*Cyperus echinatus*) * We praise you, Elder Silkgrass (*Yucca filamentosa*) * We bow before you, Elder Rice cccccccccccccccccccccccccCutgrass (*Leersia oryzoides*) * We adore you, Elder Fiveangled Dodder (*cccccccccccccccccccccccccccccccccc Cuscuta pentagona*) * We learn from you, Elder Tapered Witch Grass (*Dichanthelium acuminatum* subsp. *spretum*) * We love you, Elder Red Chokeberry (*Aronia arbutifolia*)* We worship you, Elder Virginia Wildrye (*Elymus virginicus*) * We belong to you, Elder Horsetail Spikerush (*Eleocharis equisetoides*) * We kneel bbbbbbbbbbbbbbbbbbbbbbbbbbbbbbbbbbbbbbbbbbbbbbbbbbbbbb bbbbbbbbbbbbbbbbbbbbbbbbbbefore you, Elder Hairy crcrcrcrcrcrcrcrcrcrcrcrcrcrcrcrcrcrcrcrcrcrC

rabgrass (*Digitaria sanguinalis*) * We belong to you, Elder jjjjjjjjjjjjjjjjjjjjjjjjjjJuniper Leaf

(*ppppppppppppppppppppppppppPolypremum*   *prprprprprprprprprprprprprprprprprprprprprprprprprpr*

procumbens) * We venerate you, Elder Willow Oak (*Quercus phellos*) * We belong to you, Elder bl

blblblblblblblblblblblblblblblBladderpod (*Sesbania vesicaria*) * We adore you, Elder Salt ppppp

ppppppppppppppppppppppppppppppppppppppppppppppppppppppppppppppppppppppppppppppppppppppp

ppppppppppppppppppppppppppppppppppppPennywort (*Hydrocotyle bonariensis*) * We praise

you, Elder Snake-mouth Orchid (*ppppppppppppppppppppppppppppppppppppppPogonia ophioglossoides*)

* We bow before you, Elder Whitemouth Dayflower (*Commelina erecta*) * We love you, Elder

Virginia Saltmarsh Mallow (*Kosteletzkya ppppppppppppppppppppppppppppppppppppppppppppppppppppp*

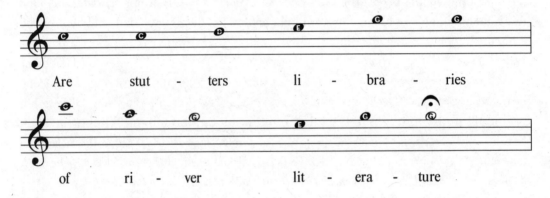

ppppppppppppppppppppppppppppppppppppppppppentacarpos*) * We belong to you, Elder Roundfruit

Hedgehyssop (*Gratiola virginiana*) * We belong to you, Elder Honey Locust (*Gleditsia trtrtrtrtr*

trtrtrtrtrtrtrtrtrtrtrtrtrtrtrtriacanthos) * We kneel before you, Elder Marsh Seedbox (*Ludwigia pp*

ppppppppppppppppppppppppppppppppppppppppppppppppppalustris) * We learn from you, Elder Path Rush

(*Juncus ttttttttttttttttttttttttttttttttenuis*) * We adore you, Elder Black Willow (*Salix nigra*) * We belong to

you, Elder Bog Rush (*Juncus marginatus*) * We bow before you, Elder Hooded pppppppppppppp

ppppppppppppppppppppppppppppppppppppppppppppppppppppppppppppppppppppppppppppppppppppp

ppppppppppppppppppppPitcherplant (*Sarracenia minor*) * We venerate you, Elder Bitter

pppppppppppppppppppppppppppPanic Grass (*Panicum amarum*) * We praise you, Elder White

Turtlehead (*chchchchchchchchchchchchchchchchchchchchchchchchchchchchchchchChelone glabra*)

* We belong to you, Elder Coralbeads (*Cocculus ccccccccccccccccccccccccccccccccccccccccccccccc*

cccccccarolinus) * We kneel before you, Elder Globe Sedge (*Cyperus crcrcrcrcrcrcrcrcrcrcrcrcrcr*

croceus) * We venerate you, Elder Scratch Daisy (*Croptilon dddddddddddddddddddddddd* *dddddddddddivaricatum*) * We adore you, Elder Slim Amaranth (*Amarathus hybridus*) * We worship you, Elder Late Goldenrod (*Solidago altissima*) * We belong to you, Elder jjjjjjjjj jjjjjjjjjjjjjjjjjjjjjjjjjjjjjjjjjjjjjjjjjjjjJusticeweed (*Eupatorium leucolepis*) * We bow before you, Elder Sharpwing Monkeyflower (*Mimulus alatus*) * We venerate you, Elder Jack in the Pulpit (*Arisaema triphyllum*) * We learn from you, eeeeeeeeeeeeeeeeeeeeeeElder Ghost Pipe (*Monotropa uniflora*) * We love you, Elder Carpetgrass (*Stenotaphrum secundatum*) * We praise you, Elder Green Amaranth (*Amaranthus viridis*) * We kneel bbbbbbbbbbbbbbbbbbbbbbbbbbb bbbbbbbbbbbbbbbbbbbbbbbbbbbbbbbbbbbbbbbbbbbbbbbbbbbbbbbbbbbbbbefore you, Elder Variable Panic Grass (*Dichanthelium ccccccccccccccccccccccccccccccccccccccccommutatum*) * We adore you, Elder Carolina Sea Lavender (*Limonium carolinianum*) * We belong to you, Elder Swamp Pink (*Calopogon tuberosus* var. *ttttttttttttuberosus*) * We venerate you, Elder Salt Sandspurry (*Spergularia salina*) * We belong to you, Elder Striped Gentian (*Gentiana villosa*) * We worship you, Elder Erect Spiderling (*bbbbbbbbbbbbbbbbbbbbbbbbbbbbbbbbbbbbbbbBoerhavia erecta*) * We worship you, Elder pppppppppppppppppppppppppppppppppppppppppppppppppppppppppp pPerennial Sandgrass (*Triplasis americana*) * We bow before you, Elder Pale-leaf Woodland Sunflower (*Helianthus strumosus*) * We kneel before you, Elder Clustered Bushmint (*Hyptis alata*) * We love you, Elder Southern Maidenhair (*Adiantum ccccccccccccccccccccccccccccccccccccc ccccccccapillus-veneris*) * We kneel before you, Elder Bear Corn (*ccccccccccccccccccccccccccccc ccccccccccccccccccccccccccccccccccccccccccccccccConopholis americana*) * We follow you, Elder Pointedleaf Ticktrtrtrtrtrtrtrtrtrtrtrtrtrtrtrtrtrefoil (*Desmodium glutinosum*) * We adore you, Elder Coastal Azalea (*Rhododendron atlanticum*) * We praise you, Elder Dwarf Witchalder (*Fothergilla gardenii*) * We worship you, Elder Carolina Redroot (*Lachnanthes ccccccccccccccccccc ccccccccccccccccccccccccccccccccaroliniana*) * We belong to you, Elder Pink Muhly Grass (*Muhlenbergia ccccccccccccccccccccccccccccccccccccccccccccccccccccccccccccccccccccccccccccccccccccccccccccccccccccccc ccccccccccccapillaris*) * We belong to you, Elder Spiniest Thistle (*Cirsium horridulum* var. *horridulum*) * We belong to you, Elder Prickly Bog Sedge (*Carex atlantica* subsp. *cccccccccccccccc cccccccccccccccccccccccccccccccccccccccccccccccccccccccccccccccccccccccccccccccccccccccccccccccccccapil lacea*) * We adore you, Elder Woolly Threeawn (*Aristida lanosa*) * We learn from you, Elder ccc ccccccccccccccccccccccccccccccccccccccccccccccccccccccccccccccccccccccccccccccccccccccccccccccccccccccc Curly Dock (*Rumex crcrcrcrcrcrcrcrcrcrcrcrcrcrcrcrcrcrcrcrcrcrcrcrcrcrcrcrcrcrcrispus*) * We kneel before you, Elder American Bur-reed (*Sparganium americanum*) * We kneel before you, Elder American Black Nightshade (*Solanum aaaaaaaaaaaaaaaaaaaaaaaaaaaamericanum*) * We worship you, Elder Aquatic Milkweed (*Asclepias pppppppppppppppppppppppppppppppppppppppppppppppppppppppppppp ppppppppppppppppppppppppppppppppppppppppppppppppperennis*) * We love you, Elder Wild Allspice

(*Lindera bbbbbbbbbbbbbbbbbbbbbbbbbbbbbbbbbbbbbbbbbbbbbbbbbbbbbbbbbbbbbbbbbenzoin*) * We praise you, Elder Fire Pink (*Silene virginica*) * We belong to you, Elder Frost Aster (*Symphyotrichum ppppppppppppppppppppppppppppppppppppppppppppppppppppppppppppppppppppppp ilosum*) * We belong to you, Elder Firewheel (*Gaillardia pppppppppppppppppppppppppppppppppppppp pppppppppppppppppppppppppppppppppppppppppulchella*) * We venerate you, Elder Tall Elephantsfoot (*Elephantopus elatus*) * We learn from you, Elder Eastern prprprprprprprprprprPrickly Pear (*Opuntia humifusa*) * We adore you, Elder chrchrchrchrchrchrchrchrchrchrchrchrchrchrchr Christmas Fern (*pppppppppppppppppppppppppppppppppppppppppppppppppppppppPolystichum aaaaa aaaaaaaaaaaaaaaaaaaaaaaaaaaaaaaaaaaaaaaaaaaaaaaaaaaaaaaaaaaaaaaaaaaaaaaaaaaaaaaaacr ostichoides*) * We kneel before you, Elder Oakleaf Fleabane (*Erigeron ququququququququ ququququququququququququququququququququququququququququququququercifolius*) * We listen to you, Elder Blue bbbbbbbbbbbbbbbbbbbbbbbbbbbbbbbbbbbbbbbbbbbbbbbbbbbbbbbbbbbbbbbbb bbbbbbbbbbbbbbbbbbbbbbbbbbbbbbbbbbbbbbbbbbbbbbbbbbbbbbbbbbbbbbbbbbbbbbbbbbbbbbbbbbbbb bbbbbbbbbbbbbbbbbbbbbbbbbbbbbbbbbbbbbbbbbbbbbbbbbbbbbbbbbbbbbbbbbbbbbbbbbbbbbbbbbbbbb bbbbbbbbbbbbbbbbbbbbbbbbbbbbbbbbbbbbbbbbbbbbbbbbbbbbbbbbbbbbbbbbbbbbbbbbbbbbbbbbbbbbb bbbbbbbbbbbbbbButterwort (*Pinguicula caerulea*) * We belong to you, Elder Smallfruit bbbb bbbbbbbbbbbbbbbbbbbbbbbbbbbbbbbbbbbbbbbbbbbbbbbbbbbbbbbbbbbbbbbbbbbbbbbbbbbbbbbbbbbbb bbbbbbbbbbbbbbbbbbbbbbbbbbbbbbbbbbbbbbbbbbbbbbbbbbbbbBeggarticks (*Bidens mitis*) * We worship you, Elder Anglepod (*Matelea gggggggggggggggggggggggggonocarpos*) * We belong to you, Elder Big Floatingheart (*Nymphoides aquatica*) * We follow you, Elder Virginia aaaaaaaaaaaaaaaaaaaaaaaaaaaaaaaaaaaaaaaaaaaaaaaaaaaaaaaaaaaaaaaaaaaaaaaaaaaaaaaaaaaaaa aaAgave (*Manfreda vvvvvvvvvvvvvvvvvvvvvvvvvvvvvvvvvvvvvvvvvvvvirginica*) * We learn from you, Elder Fern Flat Sedge (*Cyperus filicinus*) * We praise you, Elder Stiff Marsh bbbbbbbbbbbbbbb bbbbbbbbbbbbbbbbbbbbbbbbbbbbbbbbbbbbbbbbbbbbbbbbbbbbbbbbbbbbbbbbbbbbbbbbbbbbbbbbbbbbb bbbbbbbbbbbbbbbbbbbbbbbbbbbbbbbbbbbbbbbbbbbbbbbbbbbbbbbbbbbbbbbbbbbbbbbbbbbbbbbbbbbbb bbbbbbbbbbbbbbbbbbbbbbbbbbbbbbbbbbbbbbbbbbbbbbbbbbbbbbbbbbbbbbbbbbbbbbbbbbbbbbbbbbbbb bbbBedstraw (*Galium ttttttttttttttttttttttttttttttttttttttttttttttttttttttttttttinctorium*) * We belong to you, Elder Hoary Mountain Mint (*pppppppppppppppppppppppppppppppppppppppppppppppppppppppppp ppppppppppppppppppppppppppppppppppPycnanthemum incanum*) * We kneel before you, Elder Carolina ccccccccccccccccccccccccccccccccccccccccccccccccccccccccccccccccccccccccccccc ccccccccccccccccccccccccccccccccccccccccccccccccccccccccccccccccccccccccccccccccccc Canarygrass (*Phalaris ccccccccccccccccccccccccccccccccccccccccccccccaroliniana*) * We adore you, Elder Sixweeks fffffffffffffffffffffffffffffffffffffFescue (*Vulpia octoflora*) * We listen to you, Elder Anglestem bbbbbbbbbbbbbbbbbbbbbbbbbbbbbbbbbbbbbbbbbbbbbbbbbbbbbbbbbbbbbbbbbbbbbbbbbb

bbbbbbbbbbbbbbbbbbbbbbbbbbbbbbbbbbbbbbbbbbbbbbbbbbbbbbbbbbbbbbbbbbbbbbbbbbbbbbbbbbbb
bbbbbbbbbbbbbbbbbbbbbbbbbbbbbbbbbbbbbbbbbbbbbbbbbbbbbbbbbbbbbbbbbbbbbbbbbbbbbbbbbbbb
bbbbbbbbbbbbbbbbbbbbbbbbbbbbbBeaksedge (*Rhynchospora* cccccccccccccccccccccccccccccccc
ccccccccccccaduca) * We venerate you, Elder Snakeroot (*Eryngium aquaticum*) * We belong to
you, Elder bbbbbbbbbbbbbbbbbbbbbbbbbbbbbbbbbbbbbbbbbbbbbbbbbbbbbbbbbbbbbbbbbbbbbbb
bbbbbbbbbbbbbbbbbbbbbbbbbbbbbbbbbbbbbbbbbbbbbbbbbbbbbbbbbbbbbbbbbbbbbbbbbbbbbbbbbbbb
bbbbbbbbbbbbbbbbbbbbbbbbbbbbbbbbbbbbbbbbbButtonbush (*Cephalanthus occidentalis*)
* We belong to you, Elder Swamp Hornpod (*Cynoctonum sessilifolium*) * We worship you, Elder
Carolina Vetch (*Vicia* cccccccccccccccccccccccccccccccccccccccccccccccccccccccccccccccccccccc
caroliniana) * We follow you, Elder Carolina Frostweed (*crcrcrcrcrcrcrcrcrcrcrcrcrcrcrcrcrcrcrcrcrc*

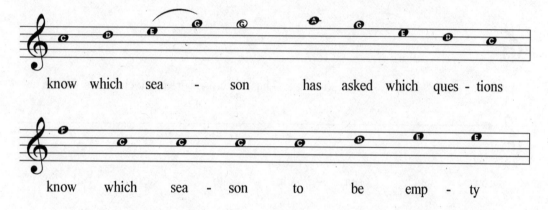

know   which   sea - son   has   asked   which   ques - tions

know   which   sea - son   to   be   emp - ty

*rcrcrcrcrcrcrcrcrcrcrcrcrcrcrcrcrcrcrcr*Crocanthemum cccccccccccccccccccccccccccccccccaroliniumum) *
We learn from you, Elder Pinewoods Rose gggggggggggggggggggggggggggggggggggggGentian
(*Sabatia gentianoides*) * We belong to you, Elder Threeway Sedge (*dddddddddddddddddddddd
ddddddddddddddddddddddddddddddddddddddddddddddddddddddddddddddddddddddddddddddddddd
dddDulichium arundinaceum*) * We kneel bbbbbbbbbbbbbbbbbbbbbbbbbbbbbbbbbbbbbbbbbbb
bbbbbbbbbbbbbbbbbbbbbbbbbbbbbbbbbbbbbbbbbbbbbbbbbbbbbbbbbbbbbbbbbbbbbbbbbbbbbbbbbbbb
bbbbbbbbbbbbbbbbbbbbbbbbbbbbbbbbbbbbbefore you, Elder Golden-club (*Orontium aaaa
aaaaaaaaquaticum*) * We praise you, Elder iiiiiiiiiiiiiiiiiiiiiiiiiiiiiiiiiiiiiiiiiiiiiiiiiiiiiiiiiiiiiiiiiiiiiii
iiiiiiiiiiiiiiiiiiiiiiiiiiiiiiiiiiiiiiiiiiiiiiiiiiiiiiiiiiiiiiiiiInnocence (*Houstonia* prprprprprprprprprpr
prprprprprprprprprprprprprprprprprprprocumbens) * We listen to you, Elder Virginia bbbbbbbb
bbbbbbbbbbbbbbbbbbbbbbbbbbbbbbbbbbbbbbbbbbbbbbbbbbbbbbbbbbbbbbbbbbbbbbbbbbbbbbbbbbbb
bbbbbbbbbbbbbbbbbbbbbbbbbbbbbbbbbbbbbbbbbbbbbbbbbbbbbbbbbbbbbbbbbbbbbbbbbbbbbbbbbbbb
bbbbbbbbbbbbbbbbbbbbbbbbbbbbbbbbbbbbbbbbbbbbbbbbbbbbbbbbbbbbbbbbbbbbbbbbbbbbbbbbbbbb

bbbbbbbbbbbbbbbbbbbbbbbbbbbbbbbbbbbbButtonweed (*Diodia virginiana*) * We adore you, Elder Roundleaf grgrgrgrgrGreenbriar (*Smilax rotundifolia*) * We belong to you, Elder Tall Horned Beaksedge (*Rhynchospora macrostachya*) * We belong to you, Elder Ten-angle ppppppppppppppppppppppppppppppppppppppppppppppppppppppppppppppppppppppppppPipew ort (*Eriocaulon ddddddddddddddddddddddddddecangulare*) * We venerate you, Elder Smooth crcrcrcrcrcrcrcrcrcrCrabgrass (*Digitaria ischaemum*) * We worship you, Elder Black Alder (*Alnus ssssssssssssssssssssssssserrulata*) * We follow you, Elder Ryebrome (*Bromus secalinus*) * We belong to you, Elder Loblolly Bay (*Gordonia lasianthus*) * We kneel bbbbbbbbbbbbbbbbbbb bbbbbbbbbbbbbbbbbbbbefore you, Elder jjjjjjjjjjjjjjjjjjjjjjjjjjjjjjjjjjjjjjjjjjjjjjjjjjjjjjjjjjjjjjjjjjjjjjjjj jjjjjjjjjjjjjjjjjjjjjjjjjjjjjjjjjjjjjjjjjjjjjjjjjjjjjjjjjjjjjjjjjjjjjjjjjjjjjjjjjjjjjjjjjjjjjjjjjjjjjjjjjjjjjjj

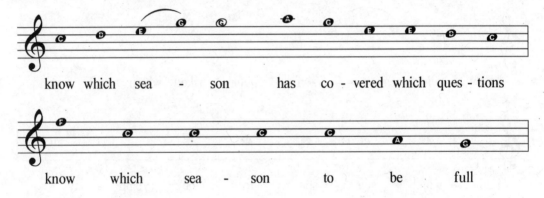

know which sea - son has co - vered which ques - tions

know which sea - son to be full

jjjjjjjjjjjjjjjjjjjjjjjjjjjjjjjjjjjjjjjjjjjjjjjjjjjjjjjjjjjjjjjjjjjjjjjjjjjjjjjjjjjjjjjjjjjjjjjjjjjjjjjjjjjjjjJuda's Bush (*Iresine rhizomatosa*) * We learn from you, Elder False flflflflflflflflflflflflflFlowering ssssssssssssSpurge (*Euphorbia ppppppppppppppppppppppppppppppppppppppppppppppppppppppppubentissima*) * We listen to you, Elder pppppppppppppppppppppppppppppppppppppppppppppppppppppppppppppppppp ppPiedmont Roseling (*cccccccccccccccccccccccccccccccccccccccccccccccccccccccccccccccccccccccccccc cccccccccccccccccccccccccCallisia rosea*) * We praise you, Elder ppppppppppppppppppppp pppppppppppppppppppppppppppppppppppppppppppppppppppppppppppppppppppppppppppppppp pppParsley Hawthorn (*crcrcrcrcrcrcrcrcrcrcrcrcrcrcrcrcrcrcrcrcrcrcrcrcrcrcrcrcrcrcrcrCrataegus marshallii*) * We belong to you, Elder Orangegrass (*Hypericum gentianoides*) * We venerate you, Elder Marsh Mermaidweed (*prprprprprprprprprprprprprprprprprprprprprprpr prprProserpinaca palustris*) * We worship you, Elder pppppppppppppppppppppppppppppppppp ppppppppppppppppppppppppppppppppppppppppppppppppppppppppppppppppppppppppppppppp pppppppppppppppppppppppppppppppPignut (*Carya glglglglglglglabra*) * We adore you, Elder clc lclclclclclclclclclclclclclClustered Black Snakeroot (*Sanicula grgrgrgrgrgrgrgrgrgrgrgrgrgrgrgrgr grgrgrgrgrgrgrgrgrgrgrgrgrgrgrgrgregaria*) * We belong to you, Elder Whiskey Grass (*Andropogon virginicus*) * We need you, Elder Box Elder (*Acer negundo*) * We kneel before you, Elder Sand Blackberry (*Rubus cccccccccccccuneifolius*) * We belong to you, Elder Yellow pppppppppppppppp ppppppppppppppppppppppppppppppppppppppppppppppppPassionflower (*pppppppppppppppppppppppppp ppppppppppppppppppppppppppppppppppppppPassiflora lutea*) * We kneel before you, Elder Downy Yellow False Foxglove (*Aureolaria vvvvvvvvvvvvvvvvvvvvvvvvvvvvvvvvvvvvvvvirginica*) * We listen to you, Elder Virginia Dayflower (*cccccccccccccccccccccccccccccccccccccccccccccccccccccccccccccccccccccccc cccccCommelina virginica*) * We follow you, Elder Yellow Nutsedge (*Cyperus eeeeeeeeeeeeeeeeeeeeeeee sculentus*) * We venerate you, Elder Elderberry (*Sambucus cccccccccccccccccccccccccanadensis*) *

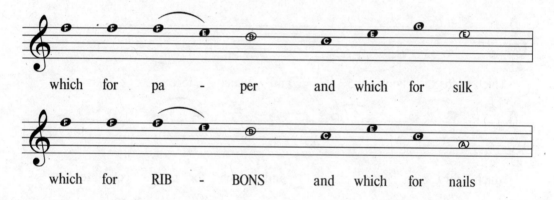

which   for   pa - per   and   which   for   silk

which   for   RIB - BONS   and   which   for   nails

We belong to you, Elder Redtop ppppppppppppppppppppppppppppppppppppppppppppppppppppppppp ppppppppppppppppppppppppppppppppppppppppppppppppppppppppppppppPanic Grass (*Pánicum rigidulum* subsp. *rigidulum*) * We praise you, Elder Water ttttttttttttttttttttttttttttTupelo (*Nyssa aaaaaaaaaaaaaaaaaaaaaaaaaaaaaquatica*) * We learn from you, Elder Carolina jjjjjjjjjjjjjjjjjjjjjjjjjjjjjjj jjjjjjjjjjjjjjjjjjjjjjjjjjjjjjjjjjjjjjjjjjJessamine (*Gelsemium sempervirens*) * We kneel before you, Elder Laurel Greenbriar (*Smilax laurifolia*) * We worship you, Elder Hornwort (*Ceratophyllum ddddd ddddddddddddddddddddddddddddddddddddddddddddddddddddddddddddemersum*) * We need you, Elder White Ash (*Fraxinus americana*) * We belong to you, Elder Carolina bbbbbbbbbbbbbbbb bbbbbbbbbbbbbbbbbbbbbbbbbbbbbbbbbbbbbbbbbbbbbbbbbbbbbbbbbbbbbbbbbbbbbbbbbbbbbbbbbbb bbbbbbbbbbbbbbbbbbbbbbbbbbbbbbbbbbbbbbbbbbbbbbbbbbbbbbbbbbbbbbbbbbbbbbbbbbbbbbbbbbbbb bbbbbbbbbbbbbbbbbbbbbbbbbbbbbbbbbbbbbbbbbbbbbbbbbbbbbbbbbbbbbbbbbbbbbbbbbbbbbbbbbbbbb bbbbbbbbbbbbbbbbbbbbbbbbbbbbbbbbbbbbbbBasswood (*Tilia americana*) * We listen to you, Elder Cigartree (*ccccccccccccccccccccccccccccccccccccccccccccccccccccccccccccccccccccccccccCata *lpa* bbbbbbbbbbbbbbbbbbbbbbbbbbbbbbbbbbbbbbbbbbbbbbbbbbbbbbbbbbbbbbbbb*bignonioides*) * We venerate you, Elder Scaly ggggggggggggggggggggggggggggggggggggggGayfeather (*Liatris squarrosa*) * We belong to you, Elder False Garlic (*Nothoscordum bivalve*) * We praise you, Elder Savanna Meadow Beauty (*Rhexia* aaaaaaaaaaaaaaaaaaaaaaa*alifanus*) * We belong to you, Elder Sensitive Fern (*Onoclea sensibilis*) * We learn from you, Elder ppppppppppppppppppppppppppppppppPink Smartweed (*pppppppppppppppppppppppppppppppppppPersicaria pensylvanica*) * We kneel before you, Elder Four O'Clock (*Mirabilis* jjjjjjjjjjjjjjjjjjjjjjjjjjjjjjjj*jalapa*) * We venerate you, Elder Florida Yellow Flax (*Linum floridanum*) * We need you, Elder Southern Nannyberry (*Viburnum rufidulum*) * We belong to you, Elder Wavyleaf bbbbbbbbbbbbbbbbbbbbbbbbbbbbbbbbbbbbbbbbbbbbbbbbbbbbbbbbbbbbbbbbbbbbbbbbbbbbbbbbbbbbbBeeblossom

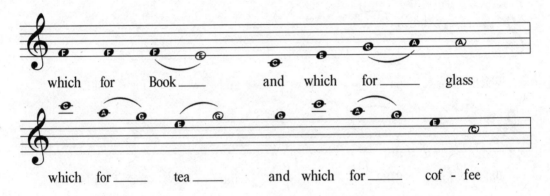

which for Book ____ and which for ____ glass

which for ____ tea ____ and which for ____ cof - fee

(*Oenothera sinuosa*) * We belong to you, Elder pppppppppppppppppppppppppppppppppppppppppppppppppppppppppppppppppppppppppppppppppppppppppppppppppppppppppPineland Milkweed (*Asclepias* oooooooooooo*bovata*) * We follow you, Elder Royal Fern (*Osmunda regalis* var. *spectabilis*) * We listen to you, Elder Woodland Lettuce (*Lactuca flori-dana*) * We belong to you, Elder Crested Yellow Orchid (*Platanthera* crcrcrcrcrcrcrcrcrcrcrcrcrcrcrcrcrcrcrcrcrcrcrcrcrcrcrcrcrcrcrcrcrcrcrcrcrcrcrcrcrcrcrcrcrcrcrcrcrcrcrcr*crista-ta*) * We praise you, Elder Hairy Lettuce (*Lactuca hirsuta*) * We venerate you, Elder Marsh St. John's Wort (*Triadenum virginicum*) * We belong to you, Elder Bent Spikerush (*eeeeeeeeeeeeeeeeeeeeEleocharis* gggggggggggg*eniculata*) * We need you, Elder Maroon Carolina Milkvine (*Matelea* cccccccccccccccccccccccc*carolinensis*) * We kneel before you, Elder Watergrass (*Bulbostylis barbata*) * We learn from you, Elder Clasping Venus' Looking-glass (*trtrtrtrtrtrtrtr trtrtrtrtrtrtrTriodanis* pppppppppppppppppppppppppppppppppppppppppppp*perfoliata*) * We belong to you, Elder Fall Witchgrass (*Digitaria* cccccccccccccccccccccccc*cognata*) * We worship you, Elder Lined Sedge

(*Carex strstrstrstrstrstrstrstriatula*) * We listen to you, Elder Fairy Moss (*Azolla caroliniana*) * We belong to you, Elder Wand pppppppppppppppppppppppppPanic Grass (*pppppppppppppppppppppppp pppppppppppppppppppppppppPanicum virgatum*) * We follow you, Elder Little Barley (*Hordeum pppp ppppppppppppppppppppppppppppppppppppppppppppppppppppppppppppppppppppppppppppppppppppppppppp pusillum*) * We venerate you, Elder hhhhhhhhhhhhhhhhhhhhhhhhHelmet-flower (*Scutellaria integrifolia*) * We need you, Elder Hairy prprprprprprprprprprprprprprprprprprprprpr Primrose Willow (*Ludwigia ppppppppppppppppppppppppppppppppppppppppppppppppppppppppppppppppp ppppppppppppppppppppppppppilosa*) * We praise you, Elder Southern Dewberry (*Rubus trtrtrtrtrtrtrtr trtrivialis*) * We belong to you, Elder Tall bbbbbbbbbbbbbbbbbbbbbbbbbbbbbbbbbbbbbbbbbbbbbbbbbb bbbbbbbbbbbbbbbbbbbbbbbbbbbbbbbbbbbbbbbbbbbbbbbbbbbbbbbbbbbbbbbbbbbbbbbbbbbbbbbbbbbbbbbbb bbbbbbbbbbbbbbbbbbbbbbbbbbbbBush-clover (*Lespedeza stuevei*) * We kneel before you, Elder Woodland Yellow Flax (*Linum vvvvvvvvvvvvvvvvvvvvvvvvvvvvvvvvvvvvvvvvvvvvvvvvvvvvvvvvvvvvvvvvvvvvv*

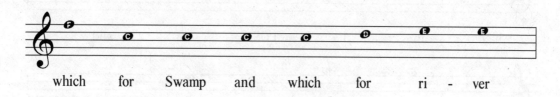

    which   for   Swamp   and   which   for   ri - ver

vvvvvvvvvvvvvvvvvvvvvvvvvvvvvvvvvvvvvvvvvvvvvvvvvvvvvvirginianum) * We learn from you, Elder Cranesbill (*Geranium maculatum*) * We belong to you, Elder Small Green Wood Orchid (*plplplplplplplplplplplplplplPlatanthera clclclclclclclclclclclclclclclavellata*) * We listen to you, Elder Cross Oak (*Quercus stststststststststststellata*) * We worship you, Elder Cottonmouth Grass (*Panicum gymnocarpon*) * We follow you, Elder Pink Thoroughwort (*Fleischmannia incarnata*) * We venerate you, Elder Sunchoke (*Helianthus tuberosus*) * We belong to you, Elder Four-leaved Allseed (*Polycarpon tttttttttttttttttttttttttttttttttttetraphyllum*) * We praise you, Elder Sparkleberry (*Vaccinium arboreum*) * We venerate you, Elder Alabama Supplejack (*Berchemia scscscscscscandens*) * We kneel before you, Elder Coppery St. John's Wort (*Hypericum ddddddddddddddddddddddddddddddddddddddddddddddddddddddddddddddddddddddddddddddddddddenticulat um*) * We belong to you, Elder Clasping Milkweed (*Asclepias amplexicaulis*) * We listen to you, Elder Blood pppppppppppppppppppppppppppppppppppppppppppppppppppppppPanic Grass (*Dichanthelium cccccccccccccccccccccccccccccccccccccccccccccccccccccccccccccccccccccccconsan guineum*) * We learn from you, Elder Whitegrass (*Leersia virginica*) * We belong tttttttttttto you, Elder Baldcypress (*ttttttttttttttttttttttttttttttttttttttttttttttttttttttttttttttttttttttttttttttttttttttttttttttttttttttttt *ttTaxodium* dddddddddddddddddddddddddddddddddddddddddddddddddddddddddddddddd ddddddddddddddddddddddddddd*distichum*) * We venerate you, Elder Little Brown Jug (*Hexastylis arifolia*) * We need you, Elder Blue Mistflower (*ccccccccccccccccccccccccccccccccConoclinium coelestinum*) * We follow you, Elder Daisy Fleabane (*Erigeron strigosus*) * We worship you, Elder bbbbbbbbbbbbbbbbbbbbbbbbbbbbbbbbbbbbbbbbbbbbbbbbbbbbbbbbbbbbbbbbbbbbbbbbbbbbbbbbb bbbbbb*Bearsfoot* (*Smallanthus uvedalia*) * We praise you, Elder Sea Purslane (*Sesuvium ppppp ppppppppppppppppppppppppppppppppppppppppppportulacastrum*) * We belong to you, Elder Fewflower Milkweed (*Asclepias lanceolata*) * We kneel before you, Elder Waterspider Bog Orchid (*Habenaria repens*) * We listen to you, Elder Swamp Honeysuckle (*rrrrrrrrrrrrrrrrrrrrr Rhododendron vvvvvvvvvvvvvvvvvvvvvvvvvvvvvvvvvviscosum*) * We belong to you, Elder Yaupon

(*Ilex vomitoria*) * We need you, Elder Tulip pppppppppppppppppppppppp*Poplar* (*Liriodendron ttttttttttttttttttttttttulipifera*) * We learn from you, Elder Saltmeadow Cordgrass (*Spartina pppppppppppppppppppppppppppatens*) * We belong to you, Elder Wavyleaf Aster (*Symphyotrichum undulatum*) * We admire you, Elder ccccccccccccccccccccccccccccccccccccccccccccccccccccccccccccc cccccccccccccccccccccccccccccccccccccccccccccccccccccccccccc*Coco-Grass* (*Cyperus rotundus*) * We follow you, Elder Silky cccccccccccccccccccccccccccccccccccccccccccccccc*Camellia* (*Stewartia malacodendron*) * We belong to you, Elder ppppppppppp*Purple* Lovegrass (*Eragrostis ssssssssssssssssssssssspectabilis*) * We worship you, Elder Two-headed Water-starwort (*ccccccccccccccccccccccccccccccccccccccccccccccccccccccccccccccccccccccccccccCallitriche hhhhhhh hhhhhhhhhhhhhhhheterophylla*) * We need you, Elder Little ququququququ*Quakinggrass* (*brbrbr brbrbrbrbrbrbrbrbrbrbrbrbrbrbrbrbrbrBriza minor*) * We listen to you, Elder Beach Dropseed (*Sporobolus virginicus*) * We kneel before you, Elder Soft Milkpea (*Galactia mollis*) * We belong to you, Elder Meadow Spike-moss (*Selaginella aaaaaaaaaaaaaaaaaaaaaaaaaaaaaaaaaaaaaaaa aaaaaaaaaaaaaaaaaaaaaaaaaaaaaaaaaaaaaapoda) * We learn from you, Elder Cutleaf Groundcherry (*Physalis angulata*) * We admire you, Elder Hooked bbbbbbbbbbbbbbbbbbbbbbbbbbbbbbb bbbbbbbbbbbbbbbbbbbbbbbbbbbbbbbbbbbbbbbbbbbbbbbbbbbbbbbbbbbbbbbbbbbbbbbbbbbbbbbbbb bbbbbbbbbbbbbbbbbbbbbbbbbbbbbbbbbbbButtercup (*Ranunculus recurvatus*) * We follow you, Elder Water Elm (*Planera aaaaaaaaaaaaaaaaaaaaaaaaaaaaaquatica*) * We belong to you, Elder Resurrection Fern (*plplplplplplplplplplplplplplplplplplplplplplplPleopeltis ppppppppppppppppp ppppppppppppppppppppppppppppppppppppppppppppppppppppppppppppppppppppppppppppppppppppppp pppppppppppppppppppppppppppppppppppppppppppppppppppppppppppppppppppppppolypodioides*) * We need you, Elder Coastal False Asphodel (*Triantha racemosa*) * We admire you, Elder Virginia Sweetspire (*Itea virginica*) * We worship you, Elder Cabbage ppppppppppppppppppppppppppppppppppppppppppppp

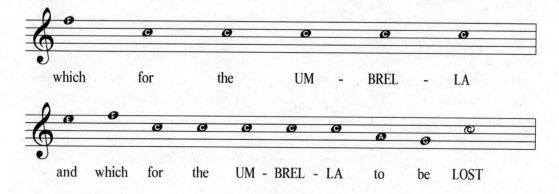

which   for   the   UM -   BREL - LA

and   which   for   the   UM - BREL - LA   to   be   LOST

ppppppppppppppppppppppppppppppppppppppppppppppppppppppppppppppppppppppppppppppppppPalmet to (*Sabal ppppppppppppppppppppppppppppppppalmetto*) * We listen to you, Elder White Fringed Orchid (*Platanthera blblblblblblblblblblblblblblblblblblblblephariglottis*) * We kneel before you, Elder American Wisteria (*Wisteria frutescens*) * We praise you, Elder Waterpod (*Hydrolea quququququququadrivalvis*) * We belong to you, Elder Ivy bbbbbbbbbbbbButtercup (*Ranunculus hederaceus*) * We learn from you, Elder Spanish Moss (*tttttttttttttttttttttttttttttttttttttttttttttttttttttTillandsia usneoides*) * We admire you, Elder Flowering Dogwood (*Cornus florida*) * We belong to you, Elder Bitternut Hickory (*Carya cccccccccccccccccccccccccccccccccccccccccccccccccccccccccccccccccccccccccc cordiformis*) * We listen to you, Elder Spiked Hoarypea (*Tephrosia spicata*) * We need you, Elder blblblblblblblblblblblblblblblblblblblblblblblblblblBluejacket (*Tradescantia ohiensis*) * We belong to you, Elder Stemless Ironweed (*Vernonia acaulis*) * We worship you, Elder Florida ppppppppppppppppppppppppppppppppppppppppppppppppppppppppppppppppppppppppppppppppppppppp ppppppppppppppppppppppppppppppppppppppppppppppppppppppppppppppppppppPaspalum (*Paspalum *floridanum*) * We kneel before you, Elder Maryland Black Snakeroot (*Sanicula marilandica*) * We praise you, eeeeeeeeeeeeeeeeeeeeeeElder Horse Sugar (*Symplocos tinctoria*) * We learn from you, Elder Virginia Dwarf Dandelion (*Krigia vvvvvvvvvvvvvirginica*) * We need you, Elder Southern Coastal Violet (*Viola septemloba*) * We belong to you, Elder Clustered Mille Graines (*Oldenlandia uniflora*) * We worship you, Elder Just Boneset (*Eupatorium ppppppp ppppppppppppppppppppppppppppppppppppppppppppppppppppperfoliatum*) * We listen to you, Elder Velvety ppppppppppppppppppppppppppppppppppppppPanic Grass (*Dichanthelium scoparium*) * We follow you, Elder White Avens (*Geum canadense*) * We admire you, Elder Neckweed (*Veronica pppppppppppppppppppppppppppppppppppppppppppppppppppppppppppppppppppppppppppppp pppppperegrina*) * We kneel before you, Elder Cranefly Orchid (*Tipularia discolor*) * We need you, Elder Rattlesnake Fern (*Botrychium virginianum*) * We admire you, Elder Starburst Flatsedge (*Cyperus plplplplplplplplplplplplplplplplplplplplplplplplplplplplplplplplplplp lplplplplplplplplplplplplukenetii*) * We belong to you, Elder Rough cccccccccccc ccccccccccCocklebur (*Xanthium strumarium* var. *glabratum*) * We worship you, Elder Greenwhite Sedge (*Carex albolutescens*) * We listen to you, Elder Netted Chain Fern (*Woodwardia areolata*) * We learn from you, Elder Scaldweed (*Cuscuta gronovii*) * We belong to you, Elder Selfheal (*Prunella vulgaris*) * We need you, Elder Marsh Flat Sedge (*Cyperus pseudovegetus*) * We kneel before you, Elder vvvvvvvvvvvVelcro Vine (*Desmodium ppppppppppppppppppppppppppppaniculatum*) * We praise you, Elder Shrubby Primrose Willow (*Ludwigia suffruticosa*) * We belong to you, Elder Three-rib Arrowgrass (*Triglochin striata*) * We bow before you, Elder Bearded Skeletongrass (*Gymnopogon ambiguus*) * We listen to you, Elder Powdery Alligator-flag (*Thalia dealbata*) * We need you, Elder Flax-leaf Whitetop (*Sericocarpus linifolius*) * We belong to you, Elder Thymeleaf ppppppppppppppppp ppppppppppppppppppppppppppppppppppppppppppppppppppppppppppppppppppppppppppppppp ppppppppppppppppppppppppppppppppppppppppppppPinweed (*Lechea minor*) * We belong to you, Elder Slender Threeseed Mercury (*Acalypha grgrgrgrgrgracilens*) * We kneel before you, Elder Openflower Witchgrass (*Dichanthelium laxiflorum*) * We praise you, Elder Lion's Foot (*prprprprprprprprprprprprprprprprprprprprprprprPrenanthes serpentaria*) * We learn from you, Elder Northern ccccccccccccccccccccccccCatalpa (*Catalpa speciosa*) * We worship you, Elder Lax Hornpod (*Mitreola pppppppppppppppppppppppppppppppppppppppppppetiolata*) * We follow you, Elder Red Bay (*Persea borbonia*) * We admire you, Elder Peelbark St. John's Wort (*Hypericum fffffffffffffffffffffffffffffffffffffffffffffffasciculatum*) * We need you, Elder Gulf Croton (*Croton ppppppppppppppppppppppppppppunctatus*) * We listen to you, Elder Bedstraw St. John's Wort (*Hypericum galioides*) * We bow before you, Elder Horse-Tail Crown Grass (*Paspalum* repens) * We belong to you, Elder Rose Vervain (*Glandularia ccccccccçccccccccccccccccccccccccc ccccccccccccccccanadensis*) * We kneel before you, Elder Saltmarsh Loosestrife (*Lythrum lineare*) * We admire you, Elder Inkberry (*Ilex glabra*) * We praise you, Elder White Wild Indigo (*Baptisia alba*) * We belong to you, Elder Spotted Pondweed (*pppppp ppppppppppppppppppppppppppppPotamogeton ppppppppppppppppppppppppppppppppppppppppppppppppp ppppppppppppppppppulcher*) * We belong to you, Elder Hairy St. John's Wort (*Hypericum setosum*) * We need you, Elder Squirreltail Fescue (*Vulpia sciurea*) * We belong to you, Elder Arrowfeather Threeawn (*Aristida ppppppppppppppppppppppppppppurpurascens*) * We listen to you, Elder Catbriar (*Smilax bona-nox*) * We belong to you, Elder Black Oak (*Quercus velutina*) * We kneel before you, Elder Sicklepod (*Senna obtusifolia*) * We follow you, Elder New York Ironweed (*Vernonia novebbbbbbbbbbbbbbbbbbbbbbbbbbbbbbbbbbbbbbbbbbbbbbbbbbbbbbbbb bbbbboracensis*) * We worship you, Elder Rose Turtlehead (*Chelone obliqua*) * We bow before you, Elder Pokeweed (*Phytolacca americana*) * We praise you, Elder Hairy PPPPPPPPPPPPPPPPPPPPPPPPPPPPPPPPPPPPPPPPPPPPPPPPPPPPPPPPPPPPPPPPPPPPPPPPPPPP ppppppppppPinweed (*Lechea mucronata*) * We need you, Elder Swamp Loosestrife (*Decodon verticillatus*) * We admire you, Elder Purple blblblblblblblblblblBladderwort (*Utricularia ppppppppppppppppppppppppppppppppppppppppppppppppppppppurpurea*) * We belong to you, Elder Trumpet Vine (*Campsis radicans*) * We listen to you, Elder Little Sweet Betsy (*trtrtrtrtrtrtrtrtrtrtrtrtrtrtrtrtrtrtrtrtrtrtrtrtrTrillium ccccccccccccccccccccccccccccccccccccccccc ccccccccccccccccuneatum*) * We belong to you, Elder Rosy cccccccccccccccccccccccccccccccccc Camphorweed (*Pluchea baccharis*) * We belong to you, Elder Sweetscent (*Pluchea odorata*) * We follow you, Elder Rabbitsfoot Grass (*pppppppppppppppppppppppppppppppppppppppp pppppppppppppppppppppppppPolypogon monspeliensis*) * We need you, Elder Smooth bbbbbbbbbbbbbbbbbbbbbbbbbBeggarticks (*Bidens laevis*) * We praise you, Elder Live Oak (*ququququququququququququququququququququQuercus virginiana*) * We learn from you, Elder Shortleaf Rose Gentian (*Sabatia brbrbrbrbrbrbrbrbrbrbrbrbrbrbrbrbrbrbrbrbrbrbrbrbr brevifolia*) * We belong to you, Elder Nodding bbbbbbbbbbbbbbbbbbbbbbbbbbBeaksedge (*Rhynchospora inexpansa*) * We belong to you, Elder Annual Phlox (*Phlox drdrdrdrdrdrdrdr drdrdrdrdrdrdrdrdrdrdrdrdrdrdrdrdrdrdrdrdrdrdrdrdrummondii*) * We kneel before you, Elder Water Hickory (*Carya aaaaaaaaaaaaaaquatica*) * We need you, Elder Swamp twtwtwtwtwtwtw twtwtwtwtwtwtwtwtwtwtwtwtwtwtwtwtwtwtwtwtwtwtwtwtwtwtwtwtwtwtwtwtwtwtwtwtwtwtwtwtwt wtwtwtwtwtwtwtwtwtwtwtwtwtwtwtwtwtwTwinflower (*Dyschoriste humistrata*) * We bow before you, Elder pppppppppppppppppppppppppppppppppppppppppppppppppppppppppppppppp PPPPPPPPPPPPPPPPPPPPPPPPPPPPPPPPPPPPPPPPPPPPPPPPPPPPPPPPPPPPPPPPPPPPPPPPPPPP

pppppppppppppppppppppppppppppppppppppppppppppppppPossumhaw (*Viburnum nudum*)*
We belong to you, Elder Shoreline Sedge (*Carex hyalinolepis*) * We admire you, Elder
Coastal Plain Willow (*Salix ccccccccccccccccccccccccccccccccccccccccccccccccccccccccccccc
cccccccccccccaroliniana*) * We praise you, Elder Comb-leaf Mermaidweed (*prprprprprprpr
prprprprprprprprprprprprprprprprprprprprprprprprprprprprprProserppppppppppppppppppppppppppppp
pinaca pectinata*) * We follow you, Elder Bloodroot (*Sanguinaria ccccccccccccccccccccccccccc
ccccccccccccccccccccccccccccccccccccccccccccccccccccccccccccccccccccccccccccccccccccccccccccc
canadensis*) * We listen to you, Elder Blackhaw (*Viburnum prprprprprprprprprprprprprprpr
prprprprprprprprprprprprunifolium*) * We belong to you, eeeeeeeeeeeeeeeeeeeeeeeeeeeeeeeeeee
eeeeeeeeeeeeeeeeeeeeeeeElder Split Bluestem (*Andropogon tttttttttttttttttttttttttttttttttttttttttttttt
tttttttttttttttttttttttttttttttttttternarius*) * We learn from you, Elder Saw-grass (*Cladium jjjjjjjjj
jjjjjjjjjjjjjjjjjjjjjjjjjjjjjjjjjjjjjjjjjjjjjjjjjjjjjjjjjjjjjjjjjjjjjjjjjjjjjjjjjjjjjjjjjjjjjjjamaicense*) * We need you, Elder
Hairy ppppppppppppppppppppppppppppppppppppppppppppppppppppppppppppppppppppppppppppppppp
ppppppppppppppPanic Grass (*Dichanthelium aaaaaaaaaaaacuminatum*) * We kneel
before you, Elder Minute Duckweed (*Lemna ppppppppppppppppppppppppppppppppppppppppppp
pppppppppppppppppppppppppppppppppppppppppppppppppppppppppppppppppppppppppppppppppppppppppp
ppppppppppppppppppppppppppppppppppppppppperpusilla*) * We bow before you, Elder Red Ash
(*Fraxinus ppppppppppppppppppppppppppppppppppppppppppppppppppppppennsylvanica*) * We belong to
you, Elder Purple False Foxglove (*Agalinis purpurea*) * We belong to you, Elder Butterfly
Weed (*Asclepias tuberosa*) * We worship you, Elder Florida Bellwort (*Uvularia floridana*) *
We praise you, Elder Poorland Flat Sedge (*Cyperus ccccccccccccccccccccccccccccccccccccccc
ccccccccccccccccccccccccccccccccccccccccccccccccccccccccccccompressus*) * We belong to you,
Elder Longhorn Bog Orchid (*Habenaria (ququququququququququququququququququququ
uququququququququququququququ)quinqueseta*) * We follow you, Elder Shallow Sedge
(*Carex lurida*) * We need you, Elder Yellow Prickly Poppy (*Argemone mexicana*) * We kneel
bbbbbbbbbbbbbbbbbbbbbbbbbbbbbbbbbbbbbbbbbbbbbbbbbefore you, Elder Turkey Tangle
Frogfruit (*Phyla nodiflora*) * We belong to you, Elder Candleberry (*ddddddddddddddddddd
ddddddddddddddddddddddddddddddddddddddddddddDitrysinia fruticosa*) * We admire you, Elder
Toothache Tree (*Zanthoxylum clava-herculis*) * We bow before you, Elder Yarrow (*Achillea
millefolium*) * We learn from you, Elder Chairmaker's Bulrush (*Schoenoplectus americanus*)
* We listen to you, Elder Longleaf Pine (*Pinus ppppppppppppppppppppppppppppppppppppppppppp
ppppppppppppppppppppppppppppppppppppppppppppppalustris*) * We praise you, Elder White
Thoroughwort (*Eupatorium album*) * We follow you, Elder Sea Oats (*Uniola ppppppppppppp
pppppppppppppppppppppppppppppppppppaniculata*) * We kneel before you, Elder Piedmont

Primrose Willow (Ludwigia arcuata) * We belong to you, Elder Bent-awn Plumegrass (*Saccharum brevibarbe* var. cccccccccccccccccccccccccccccccccccontortum) * We worship you, Elder White Mulberry (*Morus alba*) * We belong to you, Elder Bent Arm Plumegrass (*Saccharum brevibarbe* var. brbrbrbrbrbrbrbrbrbrbrbrbrbrbrbrbrbrbrbrbrbrbrbrbrbrbrbrbrevibarbe) * We belong to you, Elder Coastal Dog Fennel (*Eupatorium compositifolium*) * We listen to you, eeeeeeeeeeeeeeeeeeeeeeeeeeeeeeeeeeeeElder Buckwheat Vine (*Brunnichia ovata*) * We praise you, Elder Beaked Cornsalad (*Valerianella radiata*) * We belong to you, Elder Wild Strawberry (*Fragaria virginiana)* * We kneel before you, Elder New York Aster (*Symphyotrichum novi-belgii*) * We bow before you, Elder Devilwood (*Osmanthus aaaaaaaaaaaaamericanus*) * We follow you, Elder Taperleaf Water Horehound (*Lycopus rubellus*) * We need you, Elder Water Hemlock (*Cicuta maculata*) * We learn from you, Elder crcrcrcrcrcrcrcrcrcrcrcrcrcrcrcrcrcrcrcrcrcrcrcrcrcrCreeping Fern (*Lygodium palmatum*) * We belong to you, Elder Virginia Water Horehound (*Lycopus virginicus*) * We praise you, Elder Cherrybark Oak (*Quercus pppppppppppppagoda*) * We belong to you, Elder Scarlet Buckeye (*Aesculus pavia*) * We worship you, Elder Leather Flower (*Clematis crcrcrc rcrcrcrcrcrcrcrcrcrcrcrcrcrispa*) * We belong to you, Elder Eastern Blue-eyed Grass (*Sisyrinchium atlanticum*) * We belong to you, Elder Coastal Plain Yelloweyed Grass (*Xyris ambigua*) * We need you, Elder Big Carpetgrass (*Axonopus furcatus*) * We follow you, Elder Running Oak (*Quercus pppppppppppppppppppppppppppumila*) * We belong to you, Elder Southern Magnolia (*Magnolia grandiflora*) * We listen to you, Elder Climbing Hydrangea (*Decumaria barbara*) * We bow before you, Elder Virginia Glasswort (*Salicornia ddddddddddddddddddddddd depressa*) * We praise you, Elder Sweetbay (*Magnolia virginiana*) * We belong to you, Elder Frostweed (*Verbesina vvvvvvvvvvvvirginica*) * We belong to you, Elder Innocent-Weed (*Cenchrus longispinus*) * We kneel before you, Elder Rosemary Frostweed (*Helianthemum rosmarinifolium*) * We learn from you, Elder Low Spearwort (*Ranunculus pppppppppppppppppppppppppppppppppppppppppppppppppppppppppppppppppppppppppppppppppppppu sillus*) * We belong to you, Elder Seaside Goldenrod (*Solidago sempervirens*) * We need you, Elder Cutleaf Evening Primrose (*Oenothera laciniata*) * We worship you, Elder One-flowered Hawthorn (*crcrcrcrcrcrcrcrcrcrcrcrcrCrataegus uniflora*) * We listen to you, eeeeeeeeeeeeeeeeeeeeeeElder Shiny Woodoats (*Chasmanthium laxum*) * We belong to you, Elder Early Whitetop Fleabane (*Erigeron vernus*) * We bow before you, Elder Slender Plantain (*Plantago heterophylla*) * We kneel before you, Elder Climbing Aster (*Ampelaster carolinianus*) * We belong to you, Elder Southern Wax Myrtle (*Myrica cerifera*) * We belong to you, Elder Hackberry-leaf Goldenrod (*Solidago rugosa* var. ccccccccccccccccccccccccccccc *cccccccccccccccceltidifolia*) * We belong to you, Elder River Cane (*Arundinaria gggggggggggg gggggggggggggggggggggggggggggggggggggggggggggggggggggggggggggggggggggggggggggggigantea*) * We need you, Elder Rescue Grass (*Bromus cccccccccccccccccccccccccccccccccccccccccccccccccatharticus*) * We belong to you, Elder Southern grgrgrgrgrgrgrgrgrgrgrgrgrgrgrgrgrgrgrgrgrgrGrapefern (*bbbb bbbbbbbbbbbbbbbbbbbbbbbbbbbbbbbbbbbbbbbbbbbbbbbbbbbbbbbbbbbbbbbbbbbbbbbbbbbbbbbbbbbb bbbbbbbbbbbbbbbbbbbbbbbbbbbbbbbbbbbbbbbbbbbbbbbbbbbbbbbbbbbbbbbbbbbbbbbbbbbbbbbbbbbb bbbbbbbbbbbbbbbbbbbbbbbbbbbBotrychium bbbbbbbbbbbbbbbbbbbbbbbbbbbbbbbbbbbbbbbbbbbbbb biternatum*) * We bow bbbbbbbbbbbbbbbbbbbbbbbbbbbbbbbbbbbbbbefore you, Elder Virginia thrthrthrthrthrthrthrthrthrthrThreeseed Mercury (*Acalypha rhomboidea*) * We belong to you, Elder Claspingleaf ssssssssssssSt. John's Wort (*Hypericum gggggggggggggggg gggggggggggggggggggggggggggggggggggggggggggggggggggggggggggggggggggggggggymnanthum*) * We belong to you, Elder Laurel Oak (*ququququququququququququququququququququququququququququququ ququququququququququQuercus laurifolia*) * We belong to you, Elder Sprawling hhhhhhhhhh hHoarypea (*Tephrosia hhhhhhhhhhhhhhhhhhhhhhhhhhhhhhhhhhhhhhhhhhhhhhhhhispidula*) * We belong to you, Elder Beach Morning Glory (*Ipomoea iiiiiiiiiiiiiiiiiiiiiiiiimperati*) * We belong to you, Elder He-hhhhhhhhhhhhhhuckleberry (*Lyonia llllllllllllligustrina*) * We belong to you, Elder Philadelphia flflflflflflflflflflFleabane (*Erigeron philadelphicus*) * We belong to you, Elder prprprprprprprprprprprprprprprprprprPrickly glglglglglglglglglglglg lglglglglglglglglglGlasswort (*Salsola kali*) * We bow before you, Elder Slender ppppp pppppppppppppppppppppppppppppppppppppppppppPenstemon (*ppppppppppppppppppppppppp Penstemon australis*) * We belong to you, Elder Longleaf Lobelia (*Lobelia elongata*) * We belong to you, Elder Trailing pppppppppppppppppppppppppppppppppppppppppppppppppppp ppppppppppppppppppppppppppppppppppppppppppppppppppppppppppppppppppppppppppPearl wort (*Sagina ddddddddddddddddddddddddddddddddddddddddddddddddecumbens*) * We belong to you, Elder Silverling (*bbbbbbbbbbbbbbbbbbbbbbbbbbbbbbbbbbbbbbbbbbbbbbbbbbbbbbbbbbbb bbbbbbbbbbbbbbbbbbbbbbbbbbbbbbbbbbbbBaccharis glglglglglglglglglglglglglglglomeruliflora*) * We bow before you, Elder clclclclclClimbing hhhhhhhhhhhhhhhhhhhhhhhhhhhhhhhhhhhh Hempweed (*Mikania scandens*) * We belong to you, Elder Carolina Holly (*Ilex ambigua*) * We belong to you, Elder Hyssopleaf Thoroughwort (*Eupatorium hhhhhhhhhhhhhyssopifoli- um*) * We belong to you, Elder Hearts-a-burstin (*Euonymus americanus*) * We belong to you, Elder Spotted Horsemint (*Monarda ppppppppppppppppppppppppppppunctata*) * We belong to you, Elder Red Mulberry (*Morus rubra*) * We belong to you, Elder Shining Fetterbush (*Lyonia lucida*) * We belong to you, Elder Blackseed Speargrass (*Piptochaetium avenaceum*) * We belong to you, Elder Netleaf Leather Flower (*Clematis reticulata*) * We belong to you,

Elder Narrowleaf Silkgrass (*ppppppppppppppppppppppppppppppppppppppppppppppppppPityopsis graminifolia*) * We belong to you, Elder Cutleaf Grapefern (*Botrychium dissectum*) * We belong to you, Elder Wild Job's Tears (*Onosmodium virginianum*) * We bow before you, Elder White Beech (*Fagus grgrgrgrgrgrgrandifolia*) * We belong to you, Elder Star Chickweed (*Stellaria pubera*) * We belong to you, Elder Swamp Rose (*Rosa ppppppppppppppppppppppppppppppppppp ppppalustris*) * We belong to you, Elder Dwarf Saltwort (*Salicornia bigelovii*) * We belong to you, Elder Dune prprprprprprprprprprprprprprprprprprprprprprprprprPrickly Pear (*Opuntia pppppppppppppppppppppppppppppppppppppppusilla*) * We belong to you, Elder Virginia Groundcherry (*Physalis virginiana*) * We belong to you, Elder Pennsylvania bbbbbbbbbbbbb bbbbbbbbbbbbbbbbbbbbbbbbbbbbbbbbbbbbbbbbbbbbbbbbbbbbbbbbbbbbbbbbbbbbbbbbbbbbbbbb bbbbbbbbbbbbbbbbbbbBittercress (*Cardamine ppppppppppppppppppppppppppensylvanica*) * We belong to you, Elder Sticky Catchfly (*Silene caroliniana*) * We bow before you, Elder Carolina Clover (*Trifolium ccccccccccccccccccccccccccccccccccccccarolinianum*) * We belong to you, Elder crc rcrcrcrcrcrcrcrcrcrcrcrcrcrcrcrcrcrCrossvine (*Bignonia capreolata*) * We belong to you, Elder clclclclclclclclclclclclclclclclclclclclclclclclclclclclclclclClustered Rock-rose (*Crocanthemum ccccccccccccccccccccccccccccccccccccccccccccccccccccccccccccccccccorymbo sum*) * We belong to you, Elder Smallflower Phacelia (*Phacelia ddddddddddddddddddddd dddddddddddddddubia*) * We belong to you, Elder Spear Saltbush (*Atriplex ppppppppppppppppppppppppppppppppppppppppppatula*) * We belong to you, Elder Woolly Sunbonnets (*chchchchchChaptalia ttttttttttttttttttttttttttttttttttttomentosa*) * We belong to you, Elder Late ppp ppppppppppppppppppppppppppppppppppppppppppppppPurple Aster (*Symphyotrichum ppppppppppppppppppppppppppatens*) * We belong to you, Elder Red Milkweed (*aaaaaaaaaaaaaaaaaaaaaaaaAsclepias rubra*) * We belong to you, Elder Virginia Chain Fern (*Woodwardia virginica*) * We belong to you, Elder ccccccccccccccccccccccccccccccccccccccccc ccccccccccccccccccccccccccCarolina Laurel chchchchchchchchchchCherry (*Prunus cccccccc ccccccccccccccccccccccccccaroliniana*) * We belong to you, Elder Yellow Carolina Milkvine (*Matelea flavidula*) * We belong to you, Elder Carolina Dayflower (*Commelina ccccccccccccccccc cccccccccccccccccccccaroliniana*) * We belong to you, Elder American chchchchchchch chchchchchchchchchchchchchchchchchchchchchchchchchchchchchchchchchchchchchchchchch chchchchchchchchchchchchchchchchchchchchchchchChaffseed (*Schwalbea americana*) * We belong to you, Elder Compact ddddddddddddddddddddddddddddddddddddddddddddddddddddd ddddddddddddddddddddddddddddddddddddddddddddddddDodder (*Cuscuta ccccccccccccccccccc cccccccccccccccccccccccccccccompacta*) * We belong to you, Elder Smallflower Thoroughwort (*Eupatorium semisssssssssssssssssssssssssssssssssssssssssssssssssssssssssssssssssssssserratum*) *

IV.

ASTERING THE STUTTER

Dr. Bejoian, a speech therapist I worked with from 2012-2013, taught me a technique called *soft contact*. "If you're struggling to say a word that starts with p, b, or m, try starting the word as softly as possible," she said. Sometimes this made the syllable hard to hear. "Pause" could sound like "awes"; "brain" like "rain"; "master" like "Aster." I want to follow this softness offered by the Stutter. I am so grateful to you, Dr. Bejoian.

For most of my life, my relationship to my stutter was rooted in shame, anger, and despair. I responded to these emotions by trying, and failing, to master my stutter through various means: undergoing hypnosis; making a fist while I stuttered, opening the fist to release the word; talking in singsong; expanding my diaphragm while speaking; saying my name is "John" (my middle name) or "Shawn." Failure has led me to a grove of unknowing. If I can't master the Stutter*, what can I do? What might it mean to try to Aster my stutter?

The Prussian synantherologist (a botanist who specializes in Asteraceae, the Aster family) Christian Friedrich Lessing opens an 1829 article with the following Latin words: "Magno amore in synantherearum captus . . . ." *Seized by a great love of the Aster family*. My body has been writing a slow love song to this family my whole life—playing with Dandelions as a child, craning upward to admire giant Sunflowers, squealing as I cycle past stands of Goldenrod on a trail through the Great Dismal Swamp (a historical refuge for enslaved Ancestors).

Western science groups Plants into families based on shared physical characteristics and evolutionary history. Each family contains genera (the plural of genus) and species. Asteraceae includes Plants commonly called Asters, as well as other Plants (including Elder Dandelion, Elder Sunflower, and Elder Goldenrod—I find this a little confusing!). For most Plants in the Aster family, what appears to be a single flower (Elder Sunflower, for example) is actually a composite of much smaller flowers (hence the family's alternative name, Compositae). Each petal of Elder Sunflower is called a "ray flower"—i.e., each petal has its own reproductive structures. And the center of Elder Sunflower is composed of many tiny "disk flowers."

---

*   I sometimes distinguish between "my stutter" and "the Stutter" as a way of suggesting two ways of looking at the same thing.

123

What might it mean to try to Aster You? I want to follow these marvelously plural flowers. For most of my life I saw You only as a problem I had to fix. But working with these newspaper advertisements and writing phrases like "the stutters will be harbours," "stutters are vessels," and "stutters: a false offence," has invited me into a more plural relationship to You.

"I want you to walk up to someone on the street, or call a store, and tell them you speak with a stutter," said Dr. Bejoian in another session. This practice, known as "advertising," terrified me. I found it too intense to attempt in person, but I slowly started practicing over the phone. I would call a store, say, "Hello, I just want to let you know I speak with a stutter," and then ask what time they closed. I think doing this did help reduce my shame.

Help me stop trying to tame You. Help me let You gro wild in my throat.

One Sunday morning in February, my best friend Luísa and I were walking to church. We carried loupes—small magnifying glasses often used by jewelers. She was teaching me to use loupes as instruments of devotion. After crossing the bridge into Ghent, we stopped in front of a Tree I didn't know. She introduced the Tree to me as Elder Yaupon (*Ilex vomitoria*). Continuing up Drummond Place, we came upon Elder Hydrangea (*Hydrangea* sp.) and knelt before them on the sidewalk to examine their dried petals, gasping in delight. After about ten minutes, we turned up Colonial Avenue and encountered Elder Southern Magnolia (*Magnolia grandiflora*), kneeling again to examine Mosses and Insects nestled between the Tree's above-ground roots. We approached them so close our faces must have become invisible to passers-by. Our backs turned upward to the winter sun.

I don't know how long we stayed under Elder Southern Magnolia. Maybe twenty minutes. Eventually we stood up and walked on, knowing that at this point we had missed the service (or, that our time with the Plants was the service). A dogwalker on the other side of the street called to us: "Are you two ok?" It took both of us a beat to understand what they had said.

"Yes we're fine," I called back.

"Okay, because I just called the police. I thought you two were hurt."

"Oh. We're okay . . . " We slowed down our pace and the dogwalker walked ahead of us. They looked back at us and I held eye contact with them for some time.

When I told the dogwalker that we were fine, were they relieved? Were they actually concerned we were hurt? Why call the police? Why not approach us and ask if we needed help?

If we had waited for the police to come, how would they have responded when we told them what we were doing?

It's 2019 and I'm driving from Richmond to Dayton at night. A cop pulls me over, they come around to the passenger side, I roll down my window, they ask how I'm doing this evening. I feel that, in order to survive this encounter, I need to hide my stutter as much as possible, to avoid seeming suspicious. *Stutters: a false offence.* I succeed in speaking pretty fluently for the first part of our conversation: "You know your tail lights aren't on?"

"Ah no, sir, I didn't, I'm sorry about that."

But then they ask: "Where are you headed?"

I can feel the Stutter arriving already. *Arrival marked with water.* The Liturgy of the Name is starting, for the Liturgy happens with all names, not just my own. *Name above forehead, dock above water.* Of course, I could just say a different city in the same direction, like Cincinnati. But I choose to risk the Stutter, to step into the Clearing. *My impediment will be my Dwelling.* I stutter for a good three seconds and finally voice "Dayton." *A river of years has crossed the instant.*

Does the cop now think I'm lying or concealing something?

I look at his eyes.

"Make sure to keep those tail lights on."

In those three seconds of Stutter, who was living alongside the highway? Elder Loblolly Pine (*Pinus taeda*)? Elder Kudzu (*Pueraria montana*)? Elder Greenbrier (*Smilax* spp.)? In those three seconds of silence, did my spirit rush out to greet them? *Give me a speech impediment, that I may notice.*

Teach me to Aster You. Teach me to treat You as an Elder that has so much to teach me. I will surrender and attend to Your ensemble of blossoms. Your Dandelion Clock* will be my timekeeper. I will seek not to overcome You but to come with You; not to pray to be rid of You, but to pray for Your continued presence in my life. To stay with the mystery You steward.

What might it mean to try to Aster You? To pray that You Aster me? Instead of "I speak with a stutter," what if I "advertised" to someone by saying: "I speak with an Aster. My speech is home to a hundred blooms. These silences you may hear hold more than I could ever know. Thank you for your patience as I pause to admire their beauty."

Lessing was a stutterer. As a student of both Asters and Stutters, I look to him as my Ancestor.

Stutters and Asters are sisters.

---

* The poofy gray seedhead of Elder Dandelion (*Taraxacum officinale*) is sometimes called a Dandelion Clock.

V.

BENEDICTION, MOVEMENT 3

The choir chants:

Ancestor Neptune,

What name did you call yourself? I do not know. I honor your relationship to your own name.

I am grateful to have found this newspaper advertisement in the *Jamaica Mercury* because it allows us to encounter and commemorate you. According to the ad, you and a group of other Ancestors began a journey in November 1779, on or near land and water traditionally stewarded by, among others, the Taíno people—also known as Above Rocks, Jamaica.

The ad says you "stammer[ed] much in [your] speech." I honor and celebrate your speech.

I inherited my stutter from my mother, who is Jamaican. Did she and I inherit our stutter from you? Are you our blood Ancestor?

In Jamaica there is a saying: "mek mi ears eat Grass." It means: "Give me some peace and quiet. Some rest." The name of this silence is these Grasses in this wind.

We thank all the Plant Elders for creating the oxygen you breathed.

as mother calls to daughter
so years call to stammers

my stammers free me
from my name

my daughter ROCKS me
in the Valley
of her left shoulder

am   am   am

OCTAGON OF WATER, MOVEMENT 5

Now
unto the unknowing

a name will gro

a name will gro

a name will gro

NOTES

I used the website native-land.ca to learn about which Indigenous peoples have stewarded the land and water for the North American advertisements. This website is maintained and cared for by Native Land Digital, an Indigenous-led Canadian not-for-profit organization.

I used the following sources for the newspaper advertisements:

Daily Advertiser, January 29, 1750, https://www.runaways.gla.ac.uk/database/display/?rid=573.

Choctaw Intelligencer, February 19, 1851, https://digital.sfasu.edu/digital/collection/RSP/id/8505.

The City Gazette, April 11, 1797, https://fotm.link/d7DwS2Pbj1BRVGfqpxaWMW.

Gazetteer and New Daily Advertiser, January 15, 1768, https://www.runaways.gla.ac.uk/database/display/?rid=624.

Hodges, Graham Russell Gao, and Alan Edward Brown, *"Pretends to be Free": Runaway Slave Advertisements from Colonial and Revolutionary New York and New Jersey* (Bronx, NY: Fordham University Press, 2019), 77.

Hillsborough Recorder, May 14, 1828, http://dlas.uncg.edu/notices/notice/1141/.

"Eighteenth Century Slaves As Advertised By Their Masters," *The Journal of Negro History* 1, no. 2 (1916): 196, doi:10.2307/3035637

Brown, Thomas, and Leah Sims, *Fugitive Slave Advertisements in The City Gazette: Charleston, South Carolina, 1787-1797* (n.p.: Lexington Books, 2015), 258.

Meaders, Daniel, *Advertisements for Runaway Slaves in Virginia, 1801–1820*, 222.

Hodges and Brown, *"Pretends to be Free"*, 273.

North-carolinian, September 8, 1855, https://fotm.link/5VXiZDQqYohuGTkGaqhBht.

Liverpool General Advertiser, August 25, 1769, https://www.runaways.gla.ac.uk/database/display/?rid=489

Gazetteer and New Daily Advertiser, August 1, 1769, https://www.runaways.gla.ac.uk/database/display/?rid=778.

Brown and Sims, *Fugitive Slave Advertisements in The City Gazette*, 269.

Hodges and Brown, *"Pretends to be Free"*, 237.

Charleston Courier, April 2, 1824, https://fotm.link/NWn25Wvy3vfgznUBag8Ci.

The City Gazette, September 10, 1794, https://fotm.link/7WGTtUWJgE1V659hmEU8oQ.

Brown and Sims, *Fugitive Slave Advertisements in The City Gazette*, 99.

Chambers, Douglas B., ed., *Jamaica Runaway Slaves: 18th Century Data* (2013), distributed by Digital Library of the Caribbean, 48–49, http://ufdc.ufl.edu/AA00021144/00001.

For information about Plant Elders, I used the following sources:

Flora of North America (floranorthamerica.org)

Lady Bird Johnson Wildflower Center (wildflower.org)

Flora of Virginia (print, app and online)

Manual of the Vascular Flora of the Carolinas

New York Flora Atlas (newyork.plantatlas.usf.edu)

Botanical Society of Britain and Ireland (bsbi.org)

Wherever possible I have deferred to *Flora of North America* and Lady Bird Johnson Wildflower Center for the currently accepted scientific names of Plants.

ACKNOWLEDGMENTS

Chris Martin, Mary Austin Speaker, Tijqua Daiker, Bailey Hutchinson: thank you so much for your patience, wisdom, labor, and care throughout this process.

I also want to thank Adam Wolfond, Adjua Gargi Nzinga Greaves, Alexis Pauline Gumbs, Anita Fields, Conor Foran, Daniel Slager, Delicia Daniels, Dylan Miner, Elena Setzer, Fred Moten, Hannah Emerson, heidi andrea restrepo rhodes, James Harrison Monaco, Jennifer Morgan, Jerron Herman, Jessica Stokes, Jessica Valoris, Joanna Demkiewicz, Joël Díaz, John Ellis, John Hendrickson, Joshua St. Pierre, Katie Hill, Kelvin Ellis, Kristel Kubart, Lauren Russell, Laurie Hollinger, Luísa Black Ellis, Maria Stuart, Michael Stokes, m. nourbeSe philip, Morgan LaRocca, Pablo Barrera, Patrick Campbell, Paul Aston, Pauline Ellis, Pope Jackson, Roshaya Rodness, Sarah Dhobhany, Sarah Miles, Saskia Müller-Bastian, Shannon Blackmer, Sharon Holland, Shy Thompson, Solana Chehtman, Starr Busby, Susan Boynton, Tamara McCaw, Tyler (Crum) Ellis, and all those I've forgotten to thank.

Thanks to *Zoeglossia* for publishing "Octagon of Water, Movement 3."

Annie Forrest

JJJJJEROME ELLIS was born in 1989 to Jamaican and Grenadian immigrants. JJJJJerome lives in Tidewater, Virginia with their wife, ecologist-poet Luísa Black Ellis. JJJJJerome dreams of building a sonic bath house!

Image Description

This is a photograph of JJJJJerome Ellis. JJJJJerome stands and smiles in front of a white brick wall. They wear a white dress with yellow, light-blue, pink-orange, beige, and white flowers embroidered on it. They wear a gold chain and hold their hands behind their back. Their skin is brown and their hair and beard are black. The sun shines on their face.

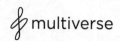 multiverse

Multiverse is a literary series devoted to different ways of languaging. It primarily emerges from the practices and creativity of neurodivergent, autistic, neuroqueer, mad, nonspeaking, and disabled cultures. The desire of Multiverse is to serially surface multiple universes of underheard language that might intersect, resonate, and aggregate toward liberatory futures. In other words, each book in the Multiverse series gestures toward a correspondence—human and more-than-human—that lovingly exceeds what is normal and normative in our society, questioning and augmenting what literary culture is, has been, and can be.

Other titles in the Multiverse series:
The Wanting Way by Adam Wolfond
The Kissing of Kissing by Hannah Emerson

milkweed
EDITIONS

Founded as a nonprofit organization in 1980, Milkweed Editions is an independent publisher. Our mission is to identify, nurture, and publish transformative literature, and build an engaged community around it.

Milkweed Editions is based in Bdé Óta Othúŋwe (Minneapolis) within Mní Sota Makhóčhe, the traditional homeland of the Dakhóta people. Residing here since time immemorial, Dakhóta people still call Mní Sota Makhóčhe home, with four federally recognized Dakhóta nations and many more Dakhóta people residing in what is now the state of Minnesota. Due to continued legacies of colonization, genocide, and forced removal, generations of Dakhóta people remain disenfranchised from their traditional homeland. Presently, Mní Sota Makhóčhe has become a refuge and home for many Indigenous nations and peoples, including seven federally recognized Ojibwe nations. We humbly encourage our readers to reflect upon the historical legacies held in the lands they occupy.

milkweed.org

Milkweed Editions, an independent nonprofit publisher, gratefully acknowledges sustaining support from our Board of Directors; the Alan B. Slifka Foundation and its president, Riva Ariella Ritvo-Slifka; the Amazon Literary Partnership; the Ballard Spahr Foundation; *Copper Nickel*; the McKnight Foundation; the National Endowment for the Arts; the National Poetry Series; and other generous contributions from foundations, corporations, and individuals. Also, this activity is made possible by the voters of Minnesota through a Minnesota State Arts Board Operating Support grant, thanks to a legislative appropriation from the arts and cultural heritage fund. For a full listing of Milkweed Editions supporters, please visit milkweed.org.

Interior design by Tijqua Daiker
Typeset in Filosophia

Filosophia was designed by Zuzana Licko for Emigre in 1996
as a contemporary interpretation of Bodoni.